NEW HOLLAND PROFESSIONAL

UPHOLSTERY

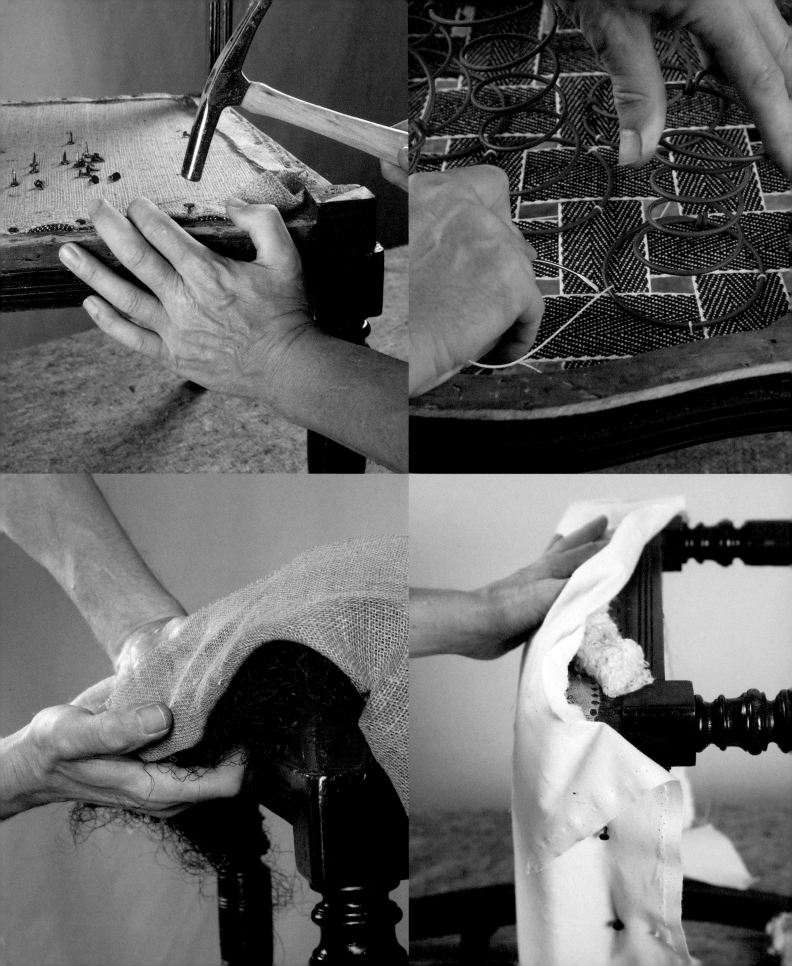

NEW HOLLAND PROFESSIONAL

UPHOLSTERY

MALCOLM HOPKINS LCGI, FAMU

NEW
HOLLAND

Dedication

I would like to dedicate this book to all those who have helped me throughout my career, and especially my wife and family who have supported me while writing this book. A special thanks also goes to the Worshipful Company of Upholders, The Association of Master Upholsterers and Soft Furnishers, and to all those students who have studied so hard to achieve their goal and in turn have provided me with a great sense of achievement.

First published in 2008 by New Holland Publishers (UK) Ltd
London · Cape Town · Sydney · Auckland

Garfield House
86–88 Edgware Road
London W2 2EA
United Kingdom
www.newhollandpublishers.com

80 McKenzie Street
Cape Town 8001
South Africa

Unit 1
66 Gibbes Street
Chatswood
NSW 2067
Australia

218 Lake Road
Northcote
Auckland
New Zealand

Copyright © 2008 text: Malcolm Hopkins
Copyright © 2008 photographs: New Holland Publishers (UK) Ltd
Copyright © 2008 New Holland Publishers (UK) Ltd

ISBN 978 1 84773 057 2

Senior Editor: Corinne Masciocchi
Photographer: Edward Allwright
Production: Marion Storz
Editorial Direction: Rosemary Wilkinson

2 4 6 8 10 9 7 5 3 1

Reproduction by Pica Digital Pte Ltd, Singapore
Printed and bound by Craft Print International Ltd, Singapore

Contents

PROJECTS

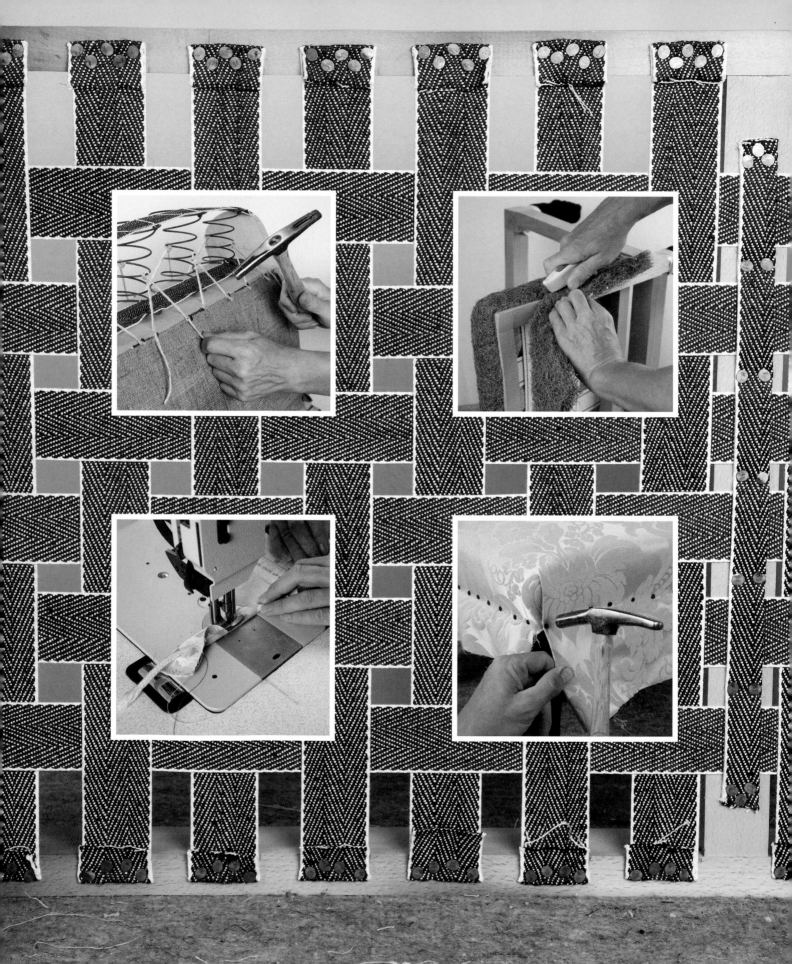

Introduction

I entered the upholstery industry directly from school where I was employed on a five-year apprenticeship under the watchful eye of Tommy Goldsmith who had already been in the industry for some forty years. Under his guidance and attending the London College of Furniture (now part of the London Metropolitan University) one day a week, I was guided through all the techniques I would need to become a fully qualified upholsterer. On completing my apprenticeship I was given two opportunities to extend my skills: the first was to work in Holland, fitting out private ocean-going yachts, the second was to return to the college and teach evening classes.

After a few years I moved on to work for a company that undertook commercial contracts, which gave me the opportunity to work with many prolific furniture designers, while at the same time taking on the training of new recruits who wished to become upholsterers. Several years down the line I returned to my roots at the London College of Furniture, this time as an upholstery lecturer, a post I have held for over twenty years.

In 1995 I was accepted as a master upholsterer in the Association of Master Upholsterers and Soft Furnishers and remain an active member of the association. In 2001 I was invited to become a Freeman of the Worshipful Company of Upholders, receiving the Association of Master Upholsterers and Soft Furnishers fellowship in 2004.

This book is aimed at those who have a keen interest in, and some previous knowledge of, upholstery and who are keen to undertake more challenging projects. The type of both traditional and modern practical projects featured here have been carefully selected to refine your skills and stretch your boundaries, and are based on the training that has been given to students at the university for nearly one hundred years. Making your own upholstered pieces is a rewarding undertaking, one that I hope will inspire you and fill you with a life-long passion.

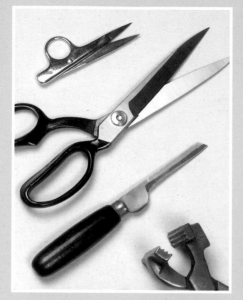

BASICS

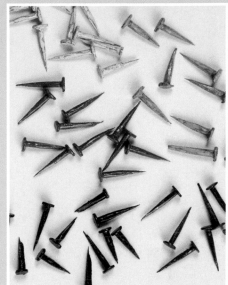

TOOLS AND EQUIPMENT

Like all artisans, upholsterers have their own personal tool kit that grows with time and experience. Listed below is a basic set of hand tools that you will need to get started. A more specialised set of tools is also outlined; these can be purchased gradually as and when required.

NEEDLE KIT

Spring needle (1)
This is a curved needle with a bayonet point to avoid damaging webbing (a packing or mattress needle is a good alternative). Is it mainly used when attaching double-cone springs.

Double-ended bayonet and buttoning needles (2)
The bayonet needle is used when stitching fibre to form an edge. The buttoning needle is used for applying buttons.

Semi-circular needle/slipping needles (3)
Available in a number of lengths and curve sizes, these needles are used for stitching where a straight needle would not be suitable. The smaller-size needles are used for hand sewing the top fabrics together when finishing a piece of furniture.

Upholstery skewers (4)
These are very large pins, ranging from 7.5–10 cm (3–4 in) in length, which enable the upholsterer to secure various types of material where tacks are unsuitable (i.e. iron-back frames or attaching calico over a second stuffing on a stitched edge).

Regulator (5)
A long, thin needle-type tool with one flat end. The pointed end is mainly used to regulate fillings (i.e. manipulate stuffing) and the flat end is used for folding pleats.

Upholstery pins (6)
Similar to dressmaker's pins, but of a thicker gauge and about 4 cm (1½ in) in length.

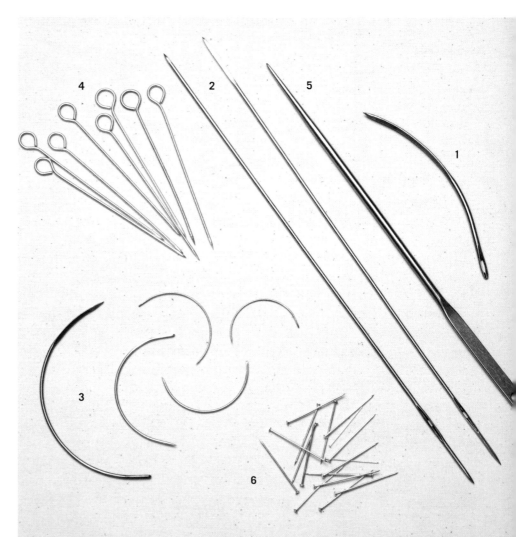

BASIC TOOLS

As with every profession, you will require a small but essential tool kit to allow you to produce all the basic forms and constructions that are required in upholstery.

Upholstery hammers (1)
Upholstery hammers have a small hitting area. Some have a magnetic or claw head in addition to a plain head, or a combination of both.

Upholstery scissors (2)
These scissors have one blade that is squared off, to prevent any accidental piercing of the fabric. It is important that the scissors are kept sharp at all times to prevent the blades catching against the fabric.

Wooden mallet (3)
A standard carpenter's wooden mallet is always used in conjunction with a ripping chisel. Hitting the mallet against the wooden or plastic end of the chisel prevents splitting and extends the life of both tools.

Ripping chisels (4)
Used for ripping out tacks when removing old upholstery. It looks like a screwdriver, except the end of the blade is ground down to form a bevel, like that of a wood chisel. Available with either a cranked or straight shaft.

Web strainer (5)
Webbing is weaved through the slot of the strainer in an S formation and the peg is passed through the slot, allowing the upholsterer to apply tension to the end of the webbing prior to fixing it in place. Various designs are available, but the bat type shown here is most commonly used.

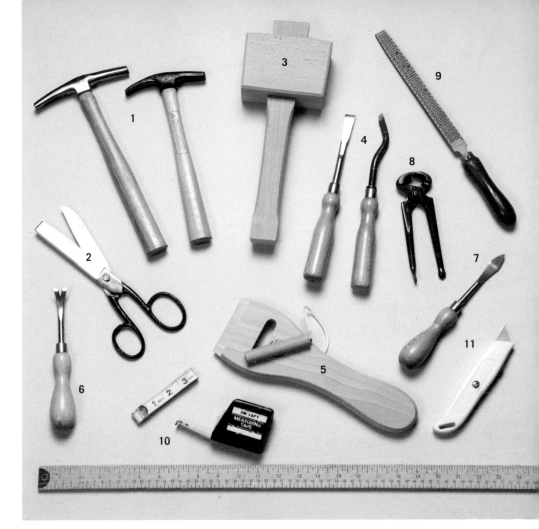

Tack lifter (6)
This tool can be used in the same way as a ripping chisel, but its use is not advisable when heavy work is required. Its two-pronged end is ideal for first grasping then lifting temporary tacks out of awkward places and when they are close to show wood.

Staple remover (7)
As the name implies, this tool removes all types of staples used within the production of upholstery. It comes in a variety of designs but they all serve the same purpose.

Pincers (8)
A form of pliers used for pulling out tacks, nails, staples, etc. Note the design of the jaws: these allow the

user to use a rocking lever motion when removing nails so that less effort is required.

Rasp (9)
Often referred to as the woodworker's file, the rasp is used to remove sharp edges from wood and to form a bevel in preparation for receiving tacks.

Tape measure and metre rule (10)
Either a fabric or metal tape measure is used for measuring surfaces on furniture in need of re-upholstering. A metre rule is useful for measuring out materials on a flat surface.

Retractable knife (11)
A standard retractable knife is useful for cutting fabric in tight corners and awkward areas that cannot be reached with regular scissors.

SPECIALISED TOOLS

The tools listed below are specialised additional tools that you will require when moving on from a basic traditional construction to more involved and modern upholstery. The various tools available to the upholsterer are powered either by electricity or compressed air, which should be supplied by a compressor. In either case great care should be taken and you should always read the manufacturer's instructions before use.

Upholstery shears (1)

Upholstery shears are like large scissors and are generally used for cutting fabric laid out on a cutting table. The shears should be of good quality and should be kept sharp along the full length of the blades, especially at the points.

Snips (2)

These small scissors are spring-loaded and hinged at one end. The ring allows the user to place the finger through the opening to provide a secure grip. Snips are used mainly in conjunction with a sewing machine to snip cotton threads.

Cabriole hammer (3)

This specialised hammer has a very small head, and it is used when working very close to show wood or tight corners. The small head enables the upholsterer to hammer in the tacks in confined spaces, preventing damage to the show wood or similar.

Hide strainers (4)
As the name implies, these are a type of both wide- and narrow-headed pliers, which allow you to grip the hide and assist in pulling it to the required position and tension.

Skiving knife (5)
This knife is used for trimming but is mostly used in the skiving of leather, to reduce its thickness.

Powered staple gun (6)
Available in manual, electric or compressed air form. The pneumatic staple gun is the best/easiest to operate during long periods. Staple guns are mainly used on modern-style upholstered furniture but are increasingly used on traditional re-upholstery, as the staples decrease the amount of force required in application compared to tacks, helping to conserve the frame.

Glue gun (7)
This tool is used to dispense hot glue where required. It is normally used to attach trimmings or gimp to upholstered furniture. The glue is very hot so care should be taken when using this tool.

Foam drills (8)
These cutters are best used in conjunction with a powered drill. They form holes in foam in preparation for the application of buttons.

Electric foam saw/cutter (9)
Used to cut varying thicknesses of foam to the required shape and size. Either a specialist version can be used, or for small jobs, a kitchen electric carving knife will suffice.

Pneumatic compressor with staple gun (10)
A variety of compressors are available to the upholstery industry. These machines produce compressed air through a control valve for a continuous supply of regulated air to the staple gun. Lower-end compressors tend to be very noisy, so make sure you take the necessary precautions and wear ear protectors at all times. Always follow the manufacturer's instructions very carefully and adhere to all regulations laid down by law in respect to the use of compressors and compressed air.

Button-making machines (11)
These expensive machines are used to make buttons covered with the upholsterer's choice of fabric. They can make various sizes of button, provided you have the right cutter and die sizes.

UPHOLSTERY SUNDRIES

This chapter looks at a selection of materials you will need to undertake the upholstery projects in this book. If you don't have a local upholstery merchant, there are countless suppliers selling a whole range of products online.

UPHOLSTERY WEBBING AND HESSIANS

Webbing and hessian come in various grades/weights. It is important to use the correct weighted webbing or hessian as these provide the main support and lining required to build the filling on.

Traditional webbing (1)
Webbing is made up of a variety of materials and comes in a number of grades. The best quality is English herringbone twill, which is more commonly known as 'black and white' and is made from flax. Lower qualities of this webbing are constructed to include a mixture of jute and cotton or hemp. Webbing is generally available in widths of 5 cm (2 in) and weighs 5 kg (11 lb) per gross (131 m/144 yards).

   The most frequently used webbing in the industry is known as brown or jute webbing, which is woven from jute. It is available in several widths and weights and the most commonly used grades are:

- 6.5 cm (2½ in)   5.68 kg (12.5 lb) per gross
- 5 cm (2 in)   4.5 kg (10 lb) per gross

Polypropylene webbing (2)
Polypropylene webbing is made from a woven plastic and is mainly used in lower-end and mass-produced furniture.

Rubber (3) and elastic webbing (4)
Rubber webbing is made from latex rubber laminated with a diagonal rayon thread which reinforces the rubber whilst allowing for stretch, resulting in a strong and resilient material. The modern equivalent of this is woven, elasticated webbing, which is constructed on a loom by weaving braided rubber cords and synthetic yarn. This produces a strong, resilient webbing and unlike rubber webbing is available in various grades for different uses. Widths available are:

- Rubber webbing   2.5–5 cm (1–2 in)
- Elasticated webbing   5 cm (2 in)

Hessians (5)
Hessian is woven from the stem of the jute plant and is supplied in several grades. The grade or weight of the hessian is determined by weighing a piece of hessian measuring 91.5 x 101.5 cm (36 x 40 in). This is known as the Dundee standard.

215 g (7½ oz) hessian: used for covering the first stuffing in preparation for stitching.
285 g (10 oz) hessian: used for lining both inside and outside the chair frame.
340 g (12 oz) hessian: this, and heavier quality hessians, are used to cover springs and other spring systems.

Scrim (6)
Scrims are used to cover the first stuffing in preparation for stitching. Unlike the 215 g (7½ oz) hessian (a cheaper substitute), scrim moulds around shapes more easily and creates a better finish. There are two types of scrim available. The first is made from flax thread and comes in two grades:
No. 7 scrim: 310 g (11 oz)
No. 2 scrim: 170 g (6 oz)

The second type is made from a very fine linen thread and is used for delicate work, such as the restoration of antique upholstery.

TACKS, PINS AND NAILS

So that the various materials used in upholstery can be fixed in to position, a variety of fixings are available, of which tacks are the best known. Tacks are not usually visible, unlike pins and nails, which come in a variety of colours and finishes.

Tacks

Blued cut tacks is the full name for tacks, 'blued' referring to the heat treatment given to tacks to help prevent rusting, and 'cut' alluding to the shape of the point. Tacks come in a range of sizes and though it is not necessary to have the complete range to hand, it is advisable to have the tacks listed below. As a general rule, tacks should be small enough not to split the wood and large enough to hold the material in place successfully without any danger of pulling away. When applying webbing to the base of an easy chair seat, the timber is usually of a heavy section. Sixteen mm (5/8 in) improved tacks may be successfully used here, whereas a drop-in loose seat would possibly only require 13 mm (1/2 in) improved tacks due to the frame being thinner and less support required.

All tacks are supplied as 'improved' or 'fine'. These terms are used to describe the thickness of the size of the head.

Above: Improved tack (left) and fine tack (right).

Tack sizes range from 6–25 mm ($\frac{5}{16}$–1 in), but the sizes and grades listed below are those most frequently used.

Upholstery nails

These decorative nails are available in various styles, designs, finishes and sizes. Styles include antique, polished or enamelled finished. Designs include round, square, multi-sided and finished plain or patterned. Sizes range from 6–25 mm ($\frac{1}{4}$–1 in). The nails tend to be sold in quantities of 250 to 1,000. For mass-produced furniture, nail head trims/strips are available which can be applied very quickly.

TACK SIZES	EXAMPLES OF USE
16 mm ($\frac{5}{8}$ in) improved	Used for fixing webbing
13 mm ($\frac{1}{2}$ in) improved	Used for fixing hessian and webbing
13 mm ($\frac{1}{2}$ in) fine	Used for fixing fabric
10 mm ($\frac{3}{8}$ in) improved	Used for fixing hessian
10 mm ($\frac{3}{8}$ in) fine	Used for fixing fabric
6 mm ($\frac{1}{4}$ in) fine	Used for fixing fabric to plywood facings

Gimp pins

Gimp pins are small nail-type pins coated in various coloured lacquers. They are used for securing top fabric where ordinary tacks would look unsightly. A coloured gimp pin will often blend with the fabric and tends not to be visible.

Buttons

Buttons used in upholstery are available in sizes ranging from 16 up to 50 on the scale system (these figures do not denote actual size; see photo below for equivalent measurements). Buttons are available with various types of fixing, some of the most common ones available are wire loop, calico tuft, nail, tape and prongs/washer.

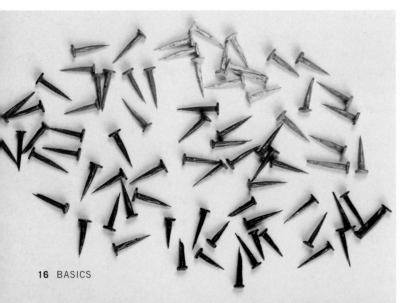

Above: Button sizes, from left to right
50 (30 mm/1$\frac{1}{4}$ in), 45 (27 mm/1$\frac{1}{8}$ in), 36 (22 mm/1$\frac{1}{3}$ in), 30 (19 mm/$\frac{3}{4}$ in), 26 (17 mm/$\frac{11}{16}$ in), 24 (15 mm/$\frac{5}{8}$ in), 22 (14 mm/$\frac{1}{2}$ in)

These materials are used for stitching, fixing or finishing. Both natural and synthetic materials are listed here.

Traditional twines (1)

Upholstery twine is usually made of hemp plus flax or jute. Twine is graded by ply – the number of strands twisted together – usually three, four or six strands. The number of strands/plies determines the thickness and the strength. The thickness of the twine is generally divided into three groups:

3-cord: can be used for light stitchwork or when a high level of strength is not required, such as stitching fabric to the upholstery when tacks cannot be used.

4-cord: used for stitching edges and the application of all types of buttoning.

6-cord: sometimes called spring twine, it is used for sewing in springs and similar heavy work.

Nylon twine (2)

Made from 100% nylon thread, nylon twine can be used for both light stitchwork and heavy work. Unlike traditional twine, which is of vegetable origin and has a tendency to rot after a period of time, the synthetic nature of nylon twine means that it retains its strength. Be advised, however, that the use of cheaper, lower grade nylon twine is not advisable.

Laid cord (3)

This is a thick cord made from hemp or flax and jute. The cord is produced by laying the fibres together with a very small amount of twist. This allows the cord to retain its strength whilst at the same time resist the amount that it will stretch.

Piping cord (4a, b and c)

Piping is available in four forms. The first two (**4a**) are made of cotton, twisted like rope and come as untreated (used in upholstery) and pre-shrunk (used in soft furnishing). It is sold in sizes, either by number (the lower the number, the thinner the cord), or as thick, medium or thin. The third cord, known as smooth piping cord (**4b**), is constructed by encasing untwisted cotton thread in encased stockinet. Finally, a variety of plastic and synthetic piping cords (**4c**) in various shapes and sizes are available for modern furniture.

Slipping thread (5)

Made from linen, this thread is used for finishing when hand sewing fabrics together. It is usually supplied in various colours and normally sold in skeins, but is also available in reel form.

Carpet thread

Similar to slipping thread but thicker as each strand contains more threads. This thick and strong thread is suitable for heavier applications and can be used when sewing folds on hessian.

LININGS

There are many types of lining. Supportive linings (hessians), intermediate linings (calico), which form and control part of the construction, and visible linings, such as seat platforms and bottom cloths, through to cambric, which provides inner cases for cushions.

Platform lining (1)

This cotton lining can be used on both the back of a seat and on the underside of a cushion to save on top fabric. When using leather this type of construction is essential, as it will allow the cushion to breathe. Sold in many qualities, the best being Bolton twill.

Cambric (2)

A closely woven wax-coated cotton material used in the making of interior cases for all feather-type cushions. The waxed surface has a slight gloss and should be used on the inner surface as it helps prevent the feathers escaping through the weave.

Calico (3)

This plainly woven cover of either unbleached or washed cotton is available in various qualities and is used as an under-covering for the better quality traditional upholstery. Whilst it is not imperative that an under-covering of calico be used, it helps form the final shape of any part of a chair to allow the easy application of the top fabric. Some believe it extends the life of the top fabric.

Barrier cloth (4)

Used as an inter-liner between the filling and any top fabric that does not comply with fire retardant regulations. Some fabrics either cannot be made or treated to achieve the required level of fire retardancy or they have a high content of natural fibre. In these cases, where allowed, the manufacturer will state that a barrier cloth is required so that the fabric conforms to the regulations. Barrier cloth is available in two types: 'non tack', which only needs to be laid on like a thin layer of filling, and a woven type which has to be fixed in a similar way to fabric, using tacks or staples.

Bottoming cloth (5)

Also known as a dust cloth, it is applied to the underside of furniture. It is mostly made of cotton or cotton mix and is usually black in colour and of a lower quality than platform lining.

Stockinet (6)

Made of either rayon or cotton, stockinet is of a knitted construction and has a great deal of elasticity. It is used as a wrapping around foam to prevent friction between the foam and the fabric, or to hold and control the layers of polyester usually wrapped around foam cushions.

FILLINGS AND STUFFINGS

Upholstery fillings and stuffings used in both traditional and modern upholstery should impart and maintain an even and comfortable surface over both the upholstered frame and spring systems. Filling materials must be able to form shape easily and to follow the contours of the profile of the frame, or of any other designs required, while at the same time filling any irregularities that may be formed by springs and other such suspensions.

The tensile strength of the materials used must be of a reasonable standard to prevent 'break up' and the materials must also provide the correct resilience to return to their original shape throughout the life of the piece of furniture.

RESILIENT AND NON-RESILIENT FILLINGS

Even non-resilient fillings have a certain amount of resilience – if they did not, the upholsterer would have great difficulty in forming the fillings and especially in applying them. Fillings can be divided into two categories:

Resilient fillings can be shaped and applied to a surface and when pressed become springy, with a soft and smooth feel. These types of filling are used in inside backs, wings, arms, cushions and full seats.

Non-resilient fillings are used for areas of bulk and for forming edges, such as over spring systems.

LOOSE AND LAYERED FILLINGS

Fillings are supplied in two forms. Loose fillings, such as fibres and horsehair, are sold by weight. These types of filling are mainly used in traditional hand-constructed upholstery. Most modern fillings, such as foam and rubberised hair, come in either layered or moulded form and are supplied in cubic volume, length or area.

> **HYGIENE**
>
> By legal requirement and in accordance with BS 1425, all fillings and stuffings must be clean and hygienic, and fillings should never be recycled from one item of furniture to another. Careful consideration should be given to this when re-upholstering and re-covering.

LOOSE FILLINGS

Over the years a wide variety of fillings have been used in the upholstery industry; some are still available, others no longer. The following loose fillings are still available and are mainly used in traditional upholstery:

Coir fibre (1)
This milk chocolate-coloured fibre is obtained from the outer husk of the coconut. It is sourced mainly from Sri Lanka but is also available from the West Indies, Thailand and the Philippines. The outer husk is removed from the fruit and is left to soak in slow-moving water for several months. This procedure, known as wet milling, swells and softens the fibres whilst at the same time removing the sap that binds them together. The fibres are then sifted to remove all debris and dirt, and left to dry in the sun, after which they are packed into bails for shipping. The fibre is mostly used in the manufacture of needle pads/mats to cover spring units in upholstered furniture.

Algerian fibre (2)
This is a much coarser stuffing than hair and should only be used as a first stuffing to form the basic shape required. It is derived from the leaves of a palm grass produced in North Africa and southern Spain where it is known as 'crin d'Afrique'. The correct botanical name for this fibre is *Chamaerops humilis*.

To produce the fibres the leaves

are first shredded by a shredding machine, then dried out in the sun and formed into ropes in the same way hair is treated. In its natural state the fibre is green but it is sometimes dyed black to sterilise it and eliminate a mite which may live in the fibre, should it not be dried before processing. Algerian fibre is able to maintain its resilience long term.

Curly black fibre (3)

Curly black fibre is derived from coir fibre and has been treated to provide a greater resilience and spring. It has in the main replaced Algerian fibre as a first stuffing.

Alva marina (4)

Derived from the southern cost of France and the Baltic this seaweed was used as a first filling in Victorian upholstery. The seaweed would in time become very brittle and dry and crack into very small flakes. It is no longer in commercial use.

Curled hair (5)

Hair is the best of all the foundation fillings. It has an almost indestructible quality, but due to the high cost of producing this filling it has been replaced by lower grade fibres. Hair is still readily available today and is sold in varying qualities, the best being horsehair, which is derived from the tail and mane. Cattle hair is also used and the hair is taken from the tails which are long in length. This type of hair is sold by weight in lengths of about 15 cm (6 in). A much lower grade derived from hog is both shorter and brittle, and much cheaper. An intermediate

Loose fillings

grade is also available which is known as mixed hair. This is a mixture of various percentages of both long and short hair. The main sources of supply are the Americas and Canada.

The treatment of the hair starts with washing to remove all foreign matter, after which it is tightly wound into ropes of approximately 24 m (80 ft) and placed in large vacuumed tanks where it is steamed. It is then hung to dry in a heated chamber to set the curl. After about two months the hair ropes are unravelled and passed through a carding machine, which contains spring-spiked drums. This pulls all the hairs apart and plumps up the hair to leave a very light mass, which can be formed into shape.

In traditional upholstered furniture

produced today, hair is mostly used as a second stuffing over the base of fibre, which is usually covered by scrim first. But at the upper end of quality furniture hair is used both as a first and second stuffing.

Feathers

Down, curled feathers and milled or chopped feathers are all used in upholstery. Down (the undercoating of duck, goose or swan), is one of the best of all feathers and is used as a cushion stuffing in the top grade of upholstered furniture. Curled feathers are a mix of poultry and waterfowl feathers, and are used in middle quality furniture. Lastly, at the lower end of the market, larger feathers are either milled or chopped for filling cushions.

NATURAL AND SYNTHETIC LAYERED FILLINGS

Layered fillings come in either sheet form or in a roll. Over the years a number of modern materials have arrived on the scene that provide similar or additional uses, but have the advantage in many cases of being suitable for use in both modern and traditional upholstery, unlike many of the traditional materials.

NATURAL FILLINGS

Mill puff (1)

In the mid 18th century, mill puff was used in upholstery and bedding. In later times, it seems likely that low-grade cotton wool was used for the same purpose and given the same label. Cotton is produced in the United States, Europe and Australia. On being picked, the cotton balls are passed through a gin, which separates the fibres from the seed. The cotton so produced is used for spinning and the remaining seeds are passed through an oil mill, which cleans the seeds and removes the shorter fibres which are unsuitable for spinning while at the same time crushes the seeds to remove the oil. The machine that completes the operation is called a linter, hence the term, cotton linters.

Woollen felt (2)

Woollen felt is produced in the same way as linter felt but the main material used is derived from the fleece of sheep, alpaca, camels, goats, hares and many other animals. Much of the felt used in the upholstery industry comes from off-cuts from other woollen goods, such as carpets and clothing. The off-cuts are torn up, carded and shredded to achieve the fibrous texture required, and then formed into a layered filling that is sold in rolls. It is also available in loose form, which lends itself well for shaping.

Cotton linter felt (3)

This is more commonly known as cotton felt, which is a thick padding. It is produced in rolls and made up from the short cotton fibres of the cotton balls, which remain after the long staple fibres are removed by the ginning process. Linter felt is available in various weights and widths for both the upholstery and bedding industries. It can be used as the final layer of filling, under the top fabric.

Skin wadding (4)

Skin wadding is formed when a layer of teased cotton fibre is sprayed with a starch to form a skin over the surface of the cotton, bonding the fibres together. Skin wadding is often used as a topping over calico, lined or open horsehair and filled items, as a means of not only creating a soft-feel finish, but to prevent hair strands protruding through the surface to the top cover. Sold by weight (i.e. 28 oz, 32 oz and 36 oz per gross) in approximately 12 yard rolls.

Interlaced padding/matting (5)

Various types of fillings (coir, fibre, sisal and horsehair) are carded and laid 'matt or batt' fashion on to a lightweight hessian base cloth, then passed through a needling machine containing rows of barbed needles. These needles force the fibres through the hessian on the downward stroke and release the fibres on the upward stroke, leaving them penetrating through the underside of the hessian. Used to a great extent in various widths in upholstery and bedding, saving time compared to applying loose fillings. Interlaced padding is used directly over spring units without the need for any additional hessian over the unit.

Natural fillings

SYNTHETIC FILLINGS

Rubberised hair (1)
This mix of short curled hair comes in sheet form of various thicknesses, ranging from 2.5–5 cm (1–2 in). The process of producing this material involves teasing or carding the hair, which is sprayed with a binder (rubber adhesive). After being weighed the hair is placed in a perforated mould where it is steamed to set and gel the binder. Finally, it is placed in an autoclave (heated chamber) to vulcanise and fully stabilise the pad. Ideal for use over arms, wings and backs and may be used in conjunction with modern spring systems.

Rubberised coir fibre (2)
This is produced using the same process as rubberised hair, although the coir fibre requires an additional curling process. It is used in the same way as rubberised hair.

Reconstituted foam (3)
This reconstituted foam, or chip foam as it is more commonly known, is the recycled off-cuts from the polyurethane foam blocks that have been converted into sheets, cushions and foam parts for furniture. The off-cuts are granulated and bonded together to form blocks from which sheets or shaped forms can be cut. Like polyurethane foam, chip foam is available in several grades: 2.3, 2.7, 3.6 and 4.5 kg (5, 6, 8 and 10 lb). In most cases reconstituted foam is used in contract furniture but it is an ideal filling for placing over serpentine springs in domestic furniture. Chip foam can also be found in banquet seating and bar stools in public houses and restaurants, wheelchair seats and church kneelers.

Polyurethane (4) and latex (5) foams
Latex and polyurethane foams are those most commonly used in upholstery. The structure of latex foam is such that it is not only resilient but permeable, too. It is produced in varying degrees of firmness or softness and can be moulded into various shapes. Flexible polyurethane and combustion modified foam is produced both in block and moulded forms and in various densities. A continuous flow process produces the foam block, which is then cut into manageable blocks. These blocks are transported to foam converters where they are cut into sheets and shapes, as required by the industry.

Polyester filling (6)
A man-made fibre derived from oil, polyester is resilient to moisture and doesn't rot. It is far less expensive than natural fillings, such as down and felt, and is available in loose form. It is commonly known as 'fibre fill' and is used to fill chair or seat cushions and scatter cushions that can be positioned for comfort. It is often used in mass-produced furniture.

Polyester wadding (7)
Polyester wadding can be less expensive than natural fillings, such as skin wadding. It is mainly used in modern upholstery, although it is also used in re-upholstery. Unlike skin wadding, it will not prevent fibres from poking through. It is ideal for covering all foams and prevents friction between the foam and the fabric. It comes in various weights, ranging from 70 g (2½ oz), used

Synthetic fillings

merely as a barrier between the foam and fabric, right up to 450 g (16 oz), used over foam to provide additional comfort and softness to the finished item.

POLYURETHANE FOAMS

GRADE	RECOMMENDED APPLICATION
RX21	Suitable for areas of light padding and headrests.
RX24	General-purpose grade for padding, arm wraps, wings and facings.
RX28	For padding and arms, giving a firmer feel over wooden rails. Used for back cushions.
RX33	Supplied in three grades of hardness. The softest is used for general-purpose quality backs and deeper seat cushions; the next level up is used to support a greater load and used for domestic seating, sprung bases and contract mattresses; finally, the hardest is used in the contract industry for firm seating in reception and office furniture.
RX39	High quality grade for office and contract seating on all types of base.
RG40	Contract seating ideal for replacement of 5 and 6 lb (2.3 and 2.7 kg) reconstituted foam where hardness is required.
RG50	Available in two grades of hardness: the softer of the two is a very dense grade for use in contract seating and domestic upholstery seating. The second grade is harder to the touch and is used in contract seating only.

FABRICS

FABRIC IDENTIFICATION

This chapter introduces you to many of the fabrics used in upholstery, some of which have been around for centuries, others quite modern. These descriptions will guide you through the maze of fabrics that are available to you.

Barrier cloth is usually a calico or wool-based cloth that has the required degree of chemical treatment to make it fire retardant. All modern upholstered furniture, or old furniture that has been re-upholstered, must be made with fabric which is either fully fire retardant, fire retardant back-coated or, if used over a fire retardant barrier cloth, the top cloth must contain a minimum of 75 per cent natural fibres, such as cotton, flax, viscose, modal, silk or wool.

Brocade is a finely woven decorative fabric that uses a variety of weaves on a jacquard loom. Patterns are formed by one or more weft threads floating on the back of the fabric which are brought through to the surface when required. The wrong side of the fabric is easy to distinguish by the floating weft threads. Brocades are rich, colourful fabrics that were traditionally made from silk, often hand embroidered, and perfected during the 16th and 17th centuries in France, Italy and Spain. Today, viscose, cotton, acetate, polyester and many blends are used to create a wide variety of fabrics used for clothing, furnishings and light- or occasional-use upholstery.

Cambric is a fine, closely-woven plain-weave fabric of cotton or linen, finished with wax, which gives it a slight shine on the wrong side. It is used to make feather cushion cases to stop the feathers from working through the fabric.

Brocatelle is a heavy figured cloth used in furnishings and upholstery, with a relief pattern, often consisting of large foliate patterns in a satin weave surrounded by a tightly woven background. Woven on a jacquard loom, the cloth has extra weft threads to pad out the pattern, producing a high relief. Satin weave forms the pattern on the warp, with a plain weft background. Originally made in silk and linen but now made using a variety of fibres.

Canvas sometimes called duck, canvas is a heavy, coarse unbleached plain-woven cotton fabric produced in a wide range of weights.

Buckram is a coarse fabric made from jute, hessian or cotton impregnated with animal glue size to give it a stiff finish.

Chenille often referred to as 'poor man's velvet', it comes from the French word for caterpillar, which is what it resembles. It is produced with a fuzzy pile-like fringe woven into the weave of the fabric in silk, viscose, cotton, wool or mixtures. Chenille fabrics are often used for furnishings and upholstery but the pile can crush to give off different shadings. It does not crease but frays easily.

Chintz is a fine, plain-woven cotton fabric, originally a painted or stained calico from India. It was used in Europe for bed covers and draperies. Especially noted was Toile de Jouy, created in France in 1760 and manufactured from 1770 to 1843 at Jouy, near Paris. Both flower motifs and the characteristic pastoral depictions and romanticised rustic courtship scenes were printed in single colours on cotton. Modern chintz is usually made up of bright prints on a light background. Today, the word chintz is used to describe any patterned or plain glazed or semi-glazed fabric used in soft furnishings.

Corduroy is a cut ribbed pile fabric with lengthways ridges or cords that may vary from fine to wide. Extra filling weft yarns float over a number of warp yarns that form either a plain weave or twill weave ground. After the fabric is woven, the floating yarns are cut and the pile is brushed and singed to produce a clear cord effect. Corded fabrics were fashionable during Victorian times, often with much heavier cords than used today. Originally a cotton fabric, it may also be made of man-made fibres such as rayon, polyester or acrylic.

Crewel fabrics are plain- or hopsack-woven natural linen or cotton background fabrics, which are embroidered in chain stitch and French knots in wool. Crewelwork fabrics were very fashionable during the 17th and 18th centuries. They depicted birds, animals and flowers and were mainly used for bed hangings. Many modern crewelwork fabrics are now made in India and are used for bedding and curtains.

Damask is a reversible, soft, glossy fabric woven on a jacquard loom to form a self-pattern. Damask is patterned by the contrast between the warp-float and weft-float fibres. True damask is a monochrome reversible fabric. Originally of silk but also wool, linen, cotton, or man-made fibres, with a pattern formed by the satin-weave background and the matt sateen-weave figuring. Traditional motifs include flowers, foliage and exotic fruits, sometimes with the addition of gold or silver threads. Fine linen table damask is one of the most beautiful examples of the modern weaver's art, in both pattern and texture. Double damask has more picks, or threads, to the inch than single damask; compound damask has one or two warps and two fillings.

Horsehair is long, coarse hair from the mane and tail of the horse. Horsehair is the weft on a warp of linen, cotton or wool and is often embroidered. The fabric is only 69 cm (27 in) wide as this is the length of the usable tail hair. Horsehair fabric is strong and very expensive.

Jacquard fabrics have intricate designs produced on a jacquard loom, invented in 1802 by Joseph-Marie Jacquard. It uses a series of punched cards to select the warp threads and to raise them when necessary, producing multi-coloured complex designs.

Dobby weave fabrics are produced on a Dobby loom, invented in 1824, which produces small, simple geometric repeat patterns.

Matelassé is from the French matelasser, meaning to quilt or wad. A matelassé is a double-woven damask fabric with a figured relief effect, which looks like machine quilting. The designs are formed by floating threads or by areas of different weaves and the stitching patterns of the back to face cloth.

Moiré is a very fine-ribbed fabric fashionable since the early 18th century. Moiré is usually silk, cotton or man-made fibres such as rayon, that have been finished by calendaring (passing between heavy iron or copper rollers) to produce a watermark on the surface. Colours are plain with a moiré lustre glinting to simulate water reflections.

Repp is a plain weave fabric with a very dominant rib running in the weft direction, with finer more numerous warp yarns. Repp is a traditional fabric produced in good quality cotton or wool for curtains, loose covers and the heavier weights for upholstery.

Tapestry the word tapestry is derived from the French word tapis, meaning carpet or covering, and refers to a heavy durable material similar in appearance to embroidery. Early tapestries were hand-made needlework fabrics produced from cotton, linen and wool, with the weft threads being threaded into the warps with fingers or a bobbin. There are different styles of tapestry cloths: many depict traditional pictorial scenes used during the Middle Ages for wall hangings, to more contemporary geometric designs. Tapestry is a heavy fabric used for upholstery and curtains. Imitation machine-made tapestries are heavy, closely-woven patterned fabrics woven on a Jacquard loom, which have an embroidered look.

Ticking is a very strong, closely woven twill cotton fabric, usually woven in narrow black and white stripes. Often used to make feather cushion cases, bolsters, pillows and mattresses.

SILKS

Silk is a natural fibre unreeled from the cocoon of the silkworm. Farmed silkworms fed on mulberry leaves produce a fine fabric. Wild silkworms which feed on oak leaves produce a coarser silk called tussah – a rough textured fabric, usually natural pale brown or stone in colour.

Doupion is a plain-woven fabric made from rough, irregular silk yarns. Doupion means a double cocoon, where silk was spun from two cocoons that were nested together and not separated in spinning. Silk stands reeled from such cocoons are very irregular. Doupions are usually made from silk but today viscose, acetate and other synthetic yarns are also used.

Satin is a very smooth fabric on the right side, produced by weaving in an interlaced pattern. The warp threads are generally much finer than the weft threads and are numerous to the square inch so that they conceal the weft and produce an unbroken, smooth and lustrous surface. Satin-weave fabrics are made from all types of yarn.

Taffeta is a smooth, plain-weave silk fabric made from evenly spaced lightweight yarns with a shiny filament, which give the fabric a sheen. Originally made of silk but now also made with man-made fibres.

VELVETS

Velvet is a soft, thick, short pile fabric, usually of silk, with a plain twill or satin weave ground. The pile surface is formed by weaving an extra set of warp threads that are looped over wires, the rods being withdrawn after the weft thread is placed, leaving a row of loops or tufts across the breadth. The loops may remain uncut, forming terry velvet, or cut automatically in machine weaving or by a special tool in hand looming. The fabric may also be woven double, face-to-face and then cut apart. Modern velvets come in many types and grades. Plush and velveteen (cotton velvet) resemble velvet and are sometimes used as substitutes; the weft loops, rather than the warp loops, form the pile on these substitutes. Gaufrage velvets have patterns produced by a heated roller stamping process.

Dralon is a synthetic fibre velvet produced in varying qualities. 'W' weave dralon is more expensive and harder wearing than 'U' weave. Dralon can be plain or figured patterned. It has good resistance to stains and moisture and is unaffected by sunlight. It does not shrink, felt or pill and is used for upholstery and furnishings.

Velour is taken from the French word for velvet and is a short warp pile cloth with a good, dense pile closely woven from cotton. Produced in several weights for curtaining and upholstery. Velour pile is laid in one direction, usually down the length of the roll, giving the surface a distinct shading.

Plush is taken from the French peluche, meaning shaggy or hairy. It is a heavy fabric with a long pile of more than 3 mm (⅛ in), produced for upholstery and some clothing. The pile is less dense than in velvet, but can be long enough to simulate fur. Plush was very popular during the first half of the 20th century as a durable wool or mohair pile cover with cotton or rayon as a base. It can be made with a warp or weft pile construction. Used in domestic and contract seating, particularly theatre and cinema seating.

Moquette (mock velvet) is a weft warp-pile fabric, which may have a cut or uncut pile or a combination of both with several colours forming designs or stripes. Very popular during the 1940s and '50s, moquette is a very durable upholstery fabric often used on public transport seating.

WOOLS

Woollen cloth has been made in a variety of types since the Middle Ages because of its good insulation qualities. After the 16th century all types of woollen and worsted products were produced on hand operated looms and later on machine operated looms. Wool is frequently combined with other fibres, including Angora goat hair, camel hair and horsehair.

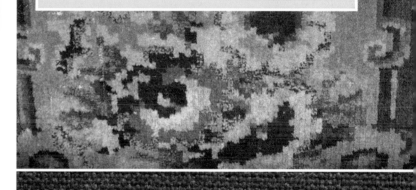

Turkey work is a woollen pile fabric, used for upholstery, made to imitate Turkish carpets. The knots of wool, generally the same as for Turkish rugs, are later clipped to form an even pile.

Tweed is generally a heavyweight all-wool cloth produced in various weaves, plain or twill, and may have a check, twill or herringbone pattern. Tweed is hard wearing and may have a smooth or rough surface. Often, the warp and weft have contrasting colours. Colours and effects are obtained by twisting together different coloured woollen fibres into two- or three-ply yarn. Harris Tweed is well known for its durability.

WHICH FABRIC SHOULD I USE?

This question requires careful consideration. The fabric used to cover any item of upholstered furniture can either make or break the piece. Several points should be taken into account before deciding which fabric to use:

• Style of the piece (traditional, modern, old or new)
• Size of the piece (large or small)
• Size of the pattern, if choosing a patterned fabric
• Type of finishing styles (deep buttoning, gathering and pleating)
• Level of usage (constant or occasional)
• Personal preference and taste

Style of the piece
In this age of contemporary designs where old and new sit side by side it is the fashion for pieces of traditional furniture to be covered in modern looking fabrics. Applying a highly patterned, brightly coloured printed fabric to a Victorian-style chair, which would have originally been covered in a cotton velvet, can enhance the older style of furniture, but of course it is all down to personal taste.

Size of the piece and fabric pattern
When choosing fabrics the choice of colour should be defined by a number of factors: the room the upholstered item is to be placed in and the surrounding colours and materials it has to blend with, such as any polished or painted wood that is part of the piece. Also, when choosing a fabric with a pattern, careful attention should be given

to the size of the pattern – a small pattern on a large chair, for example, will, in nearly all cases, work well, whereas a large motif on a small chair could result in the visual effect of the pattern being lost. Further consideration should also be given to the pattern drop (the length of the pattern), which can, in rare cases, be as much as two metres (2¼ yards). This may result in the piece needing vast amounts of fabric and an excess of wastage.

Type of finishing styles
Fabric is applied in a variety of styles: deep buttoning, gathering and pleating. It is important to choose not only the right style of application but the right fabric, too, so that they work in harmony with the piece to be upholstered. For instance, a striped or chequered fabric will look distorted or unbalanced if used for deep buttoning. The same applies if using a large pattern, which would become distorted to the extent of no longer being identifiable. Choose a plain fabric or one with a small, regular pattern when deep buttoning. Equally, a minor adjustment to the height and/or width of the diamonds could be made to give the impression that each diamond has its own central pattern.
If overdone, gathering and pleating can have an adverse effect on the finished appearance of the upholstered piece. But in most cases gathering or pleating (or a combination of both) is usually restricted to small areas, such as the front of arms and/or seat corners.

Level of usage
This should be very carefully considered, as only you or your customer knows how much the upholstered item will be used and where it will be positioned. In all cases, reference should be made to the fabric manufacturer's guidelines, which will state what the fabric can be used for. From the upholsterer's point of view, the fabric should reach the latest fire and safety requirements.

Personal preference and taste
Personal tastes cannot be accounted for but it is an idea to consult a qualified upholsterer before you purchase your fabric. If you have something in mind, discuss it with your upholsterer who should explain the pros and cons of a particular fabric choice – being fully aware of all the facts will prevent disappointment in the long run!

ESTIMATING FABRIC QUANTITIES

Any upholstery project you undertake will require you to calculate the amount of fabric needed to cover the item of furniture. If calculating for a simple set of dining chairs, then it is fairly straightforward, but when it comes to working out quantities for larger items, such as armchairs or sofas, which are made up of a dozen or more pieces of fabric, it can become very confusing. The simple steps below will help you to successfully estimate the amount of fabric required.

Assimilating the facts

When re-upholstering an armchair for instance, make yourself fully aware of where each piece of fabric is positioned, as well as how and where it is attached to the frame. In some cases you may be required to physically examine it by sliding your hand between the arm and the seat. Be careful when pushing your hand between the arm and seat as objects get lost in these voids and can cause injury.

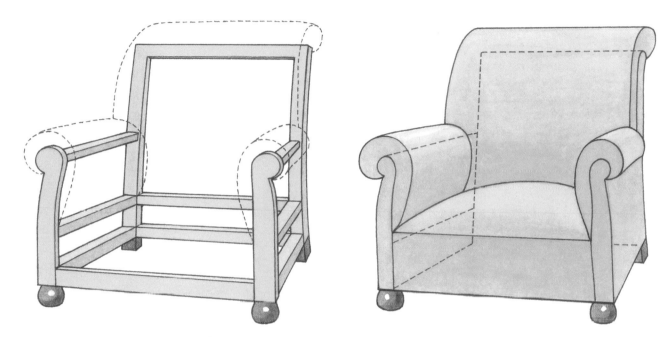

Above: These drawings show the same armchair as a bare frame (left) and as a fully upholstered item (right).

Take notes and/or photographs of how the fabric you are about to remove has been applied, taking into account the pattern layout and position, and if relevant, the direction of the pile (shown here by the red arrows). Consider the possibility that there is a reason why the fabric has been applied in a particular way.

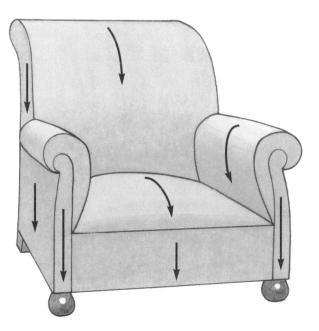

When satisfied that you have gathered enough information, start to draw up a list of sizes. This list should clearly identify each and every panel and how many of each there are. When measuring it is important that you take the measurements in a particular order: the height or depth first, followed by the width. Don't worry about shaping at this stage – just measure the greatest depth and width of each panel. Doing this will ensure that when you come to mark out and cut the fabric, the pile or pattern will run in the right direction. Remember, measure twice cut once!

The cutting plan (for plain fabric)
You are now ready to produce a combined estimation and cutting plan. For this, work with rectangles only and do not worry about any shaping. The plan that is displayed here assumes you are working with a plain fabric. Start by studying the various panels on your list and begin to position those that require the full width of the fabric and those where two or more panels make up the width. It is often the case with pairs of fabric panels, such as inside arms, that they will both fit into the full width of the fabric. When you are no longer able to place panels side by side, position the largest of the panels, then follow with the remaining panels, decreasing in width as you continue down the plan until all panels have been accounted for. This may leave you with a long section of narrow fabric on one side, which will provide you with enough material for self-piping.

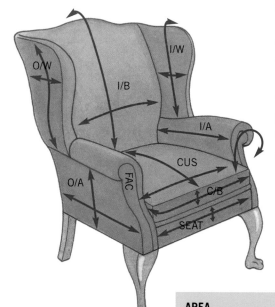

TIP: Clearly identify areas of the chair that may have two or more parts. Don't get caught short of fabric by only allowing for one arm or wing!

AREA	KEY	PANELS
Inside arm	(I/A)	2
Inside wing	(I/W)	2
Inside back	(I/B)	1
Outside arm	(O/A)	2
Outside back	(O/B)	1
Outside wing	(O/W)	2
Seat	(SEAT)	1
Cushion top/bottom	(CUS)	2
Cushion borders	(C/B)	2 widths
Cushion zip border	(ZIP)	1 width cut in 2
Arm Facings	(FAC)	2
Piping	(PIPING)	Total length req.

Cutting plan diagram:

- 68 cm / W: 66cm — CUS
- W: 66cm — CUS
- 10 cm / C/B — W: 200 cm
- 10 cm / C/B — W: 200 cm
- 7 cm — Zip/B
- 60 cm / I/A — W: 68 cm
- I/A — W: 68 cm
- 90 cm / W: 73 cm — I/B
- 86 cm / W: 63 cm — O/B
- 76 cm / W: 68 cm — SEAT
- 51 cm / W: 48 cm — I/W
- 51 cm / W: 48 cm — I/W
- 40 cm / W: 71 cm — O/A
- FAC 12 cm / 50 cm / W: 40 cm — O/W
- 40 cm / W: 71 cm — O/A
- FAC 12 cm / 50 cm / W: 40 cm — O/W
- PIPING 12 m
- 75 cm

Fabric width: 137 cm

Total fabric length: 4.76 m

The cutting plan (for patterned fabric)

Drawing up a cutting plan for patterned fabric works in very much the same way as for plain fabric but there are some extra pointers to consider, such as the pattern drop and the positioning of the pattern on the fabric. Carefully measure all panels and list them according to size. I have chosen a Victorian spoon back armchair as an example here. As you can see by the two estimation plans there is quite a difference in the amount of material required – this is often the case when upholstering a single chair – but where many panels are required the pattern can be utilised by mixing the different size panels to reduce wastage.

Sometimes it is difficult and time consuming to produce an accurate estimation plan with patterned fabric. For instance: If you require ten panels half the width of the fabric with a drop of 55 cm (21½ in) and the pattern drop is 60 cm (23½ in) you would have to purchase 6 metres (6.5 yards) rather than 5.5 metres (6 yards) of fabric.

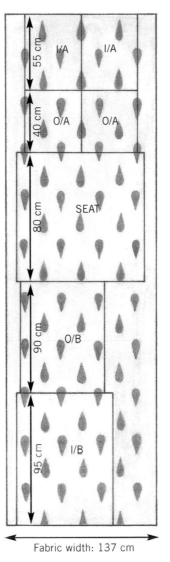

Cutting plan for patterned fabric

Fabric width: 137 cm

Total fabric length: 3.60 m

Cutting plan for plain fabric

Fabric width: 137 cm

Total fabric length: 2.74 m

WORKING WITH PATTERNED FABRIC
When using patterned fabric, the repeat of the pattern (known as the pattern drop) can vary from as little as 5 cm (2 in) up to 150 cm (4 ft 9 in) and sometimes more. You should also bear in mind that the pattern is sometimes not printed or woven centrally on the width of the fabric. This, along with checking for colour consistency, quantity supplied and any faults in the fabric should be done prior to marking and especially cutting the fabric.

If you had several panel sizes of full and half width and of various heights/depths, then it may be possible to work out your estimation plan so as to apply the panels in a particular order. For instance, some sofa and chair cushions, if cut as individual panels, will likely require additional material as wastage will accumulate between each panel because of the pattern. Cutting the panels in a particular order, as the diagram on the right demonstrates, not only reduces wastage but also allows the pattern to automatically flow onto each panel.

Nowadays there are various computer programs that enable you to estimate the amount of fabric required, but with a little practice and experience you will be able to judge these quantities for yourself.

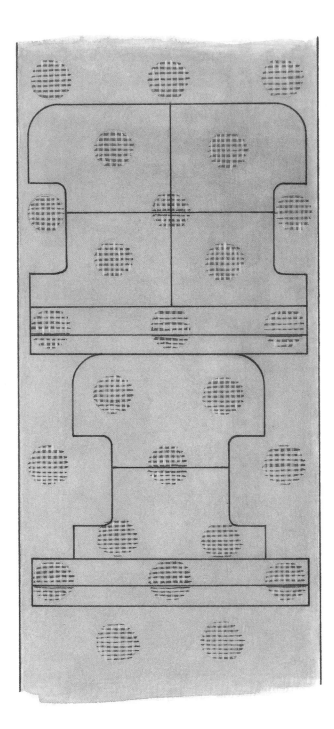

Above: When working with patterned fabrics, it is important to carefully work out where each panel will be placed to accommodate the flow of the pattern.

Reducing the amount of fabric required

One method used by upholsterers to reduce the quantity of fabric required is to use 'flies'. Flies are extensions of material that are sewn to the fabric being applied that will not be visible when the chair is completed. Flies can be of any suitable material as long as it is new and meets the current fire regulations. The diagram shows an inside back that has been constructed to be capped on with scroll facings, a collar (sometimes known as a fitted fly), using a self fabric and a fly. When a fly is used and there is no chance of the customer seeing it, a substitute fabric can be used instead.

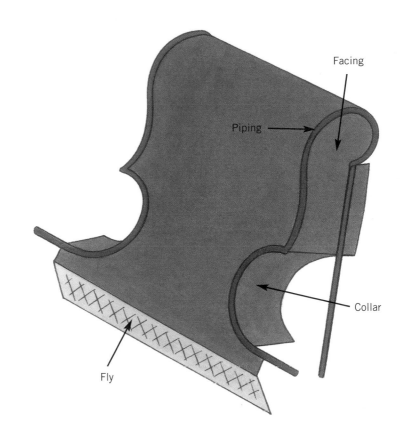

MEASURING FOR FABRICS OVER AN UNEVEN SURFACE OR SHAPE

This simple drawing describes how, by taking a series of measurements over an uneven surface, such as a sprung dining chair that is up to the stuffing stage, you can cut a piece of hessian or scrim economically.

If making a set of matching dining chairs, make sure that each piece of hessian/scrim is cut to the same size. Tack it down in exactly the same way on each chair – this will help the upholsterer maintain the same finished seat height on a matching set of chairs.

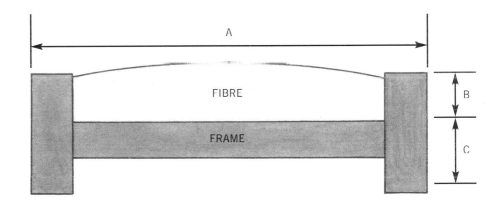

A = Measure the width of the upholstery frame at its widest point if shaped.

B = Measure the height of the finished upholstered part of the chair. This measurement should be doubled if the chair has a stitched edge on both sides.

C = This measurement is required for tacking purposes. It is usually approximately 7 cm (2¾ in). This measurement should be doubled if the chair has a stitched edge on both sides.

Therefore, in this example, the width of material required is worked out by adding together A + B (x 2) + C (x 2). This is the total width of hessian or scrim required.

Repeat this formula to calculate the depth.

TECHNIQUES

RIPPING OR STRIPPING DOWN

Before you start working on a piece of upholstered furniture, like a chair for instance, you will need to decide if you want to remove all fabrics, fillings and springs or if you are just going to renovate it, in which case you will only need to remove the fabric and/or those parts of the chair that may need repairing or replacing. Your main concern is to ensure minimum damage to the frame, especially to polished or painted areas. Care should be taken near the joints. Many, if not all, old frames are held together with animal glue and over the years, especially in modern centrally-heated homes, the glue has become very dry and crystallised, resulting in the joints being held together by the upholstery only, which when removed separates the joints from the body of the frame and in extreme cases causes the whole frame to fall apart.

TOOLS

The tools listed below are those required for the removal of upholstered materials:

Upholstery shears **(1)**
Various knifes **(2)**
Mallet **(3)**
Tack lifter **(4)**
Various staple removers **(5)**
Upholstery hammer **(6)**
Various styles of ripping chisels **(7)**
Pliers **(8)**
Pincers **(9)**

Before you start ripping or stripping down, you may wish to take a few photographs or make a few sketches to use as a reference. Take a good look at the item in question, a chair for example, and consider the following points:

• Estimate the amount of fabric you require now as once removed you may no longer get a clear picture of how each piece is linked together.
• Take vital measurements, such as the height of the seat, the diameter, the width of the arm and the thickness of the inside back. All this information could be lost once the chair is stripped.
• If you are replacing part or all of the fillings and spring systems, record all the information you need now. This will help you to correctly re-upholster the chair. You should make notes of the height and gauge of the springs in the various parts of the chair and how many webs support the springs. Does the chair have some form of mechanism? Is there something special in the way the upholstery is constructed? For instance, was the frame made whole or was it partially upholstered in pieces and then assembled? This is known knock down furniture (KD).

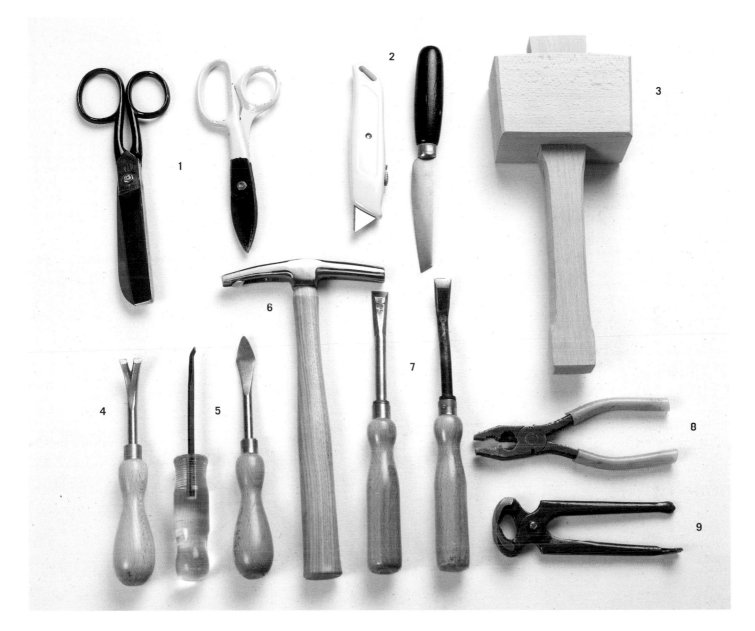

• It is in your interest to photograph the chair before, during ripping down and during its reconstruction. This will help you to fully understand the various layers that make up the chair.

• Keep all the fabric you are removing so that you can refer back to it when you are re-upholstering the chair. It may be worth retaining small parts of the old upholstery, such as the front of the arm, for future reference. Remember you can always dispose of these materials after you have completed the chair.

■ When removing old upholstery, whether on a small drop-in loose seat or a buttoned wing chair, your first priority is your own health and safety. If working on a small item such as a drop-in seat, clamp or tie it to a workbench so that when it is struck with a mallet and chisel, its movement is restricted and it will not fly off the bench and injure you. When working on a larger item of furniture, such as a chair, place it upside down to remove all the materials and tacks from the underside. The chair will need to be rotated in to various positions during the removal process. Make sure you take all the necessary precautions when lifting heavy or large objects.

The furniture you rip down may be very old and dusty, so wear a dust mask and take care when putting your hands between the seat, back and arms in case you come across any sharp objects. It is good practice to remove one layer at a time in the reverse order that you would re-upholster a chair. For guidance I have listed the order in which the materials should be removed. The order is based on a wing chair:

1) Bottom cloth
2) Outside back
3) Outside arm
4) Seat
5) Inside back /wings (the removal of these parts can be reversed according to how they have been tacked down)
6) Arms

Start by removing the bottom cloth. Use the ripping chisel and mallet to lift the tacks from the rail, and, for safety reasons always hit away from yourself. Hit in the direction of the grain to prevent the wood from splitting. If working on a chair, you would remove all outside panels before moving on.

Follow the same procedure to remove the seat cover, taking care not to damage any show wood.

Remove the top fillings, release the scrim and cut the bridal ties to release the stuffing from the body of the seat. Once the stuffing has come out, the spring hessian can be released from the springs and discarded. Then remove the spring lashings, and cut the twine holding the springs to the webbing. Finally, unfix the webbing.

WEBBING

There are several types of webbing and they fall into two categories: traditional and modern. Traditional webbing is almost always made from natural materials such as jute and flax whereas modern webbing is constructed from a variety of materials both synthetic and natural.

TRADITIONAL WEBBING

Traditional webbing such as jute or flax provides a foundation for suspension systems and/or fillings to be attached to. The type of support/suspension required determines the number of webs needed. It is important to correctly work out the number of webs required and their layout on any frame to be upholstered.

Example 1: A drop-in loose seat where the webbing is attached to the topside of the rail requires a U pattern of application in the order of four-three-two, using 13 mm (½ in) improved tacks. This means that each web is placed with a 3 cm (1¼ in) fold on one rail and has four tacks applied. The web is then stretched to the opposite rail where three tacks are inserted. It is then cut, allowing for a 3 cm (1¼ in) fold, and tacked down with two tacks.

Example 2: A full-size armchair will have a sprung seat with the webs applied on the underside of the frame. Unlike the drop-in loose seat where the frame will carry only some of the weight and strain of a person, this type of construction requires the webbing to carry all the weight and tension of the springs. It will therefore need to be fixed more securely. This is done by using a five-four-three pattern and 16 mm (⅝ in) improved tacks in a W formation.

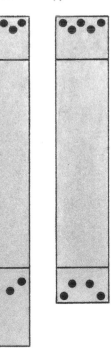

Example 1:
U pattern of application

Example 2:
W pattern of application

APPLYING WEBBING TO THE FRAME

When applying jute or similar webbing to an upholstery frame it is essential to consider the following three points:

• Spacing of webs

Assuming the webbing is 5 cm (2 in) wide in the following seat constructions the spacing required between the webbing should be:

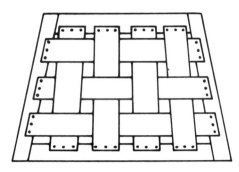

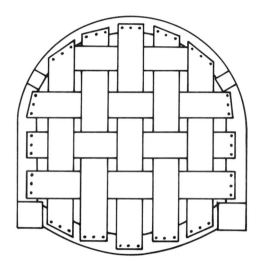

Drop-in seat

Webs covered by hessian only should be placed a maximum of 5 cm (2 in) apart.

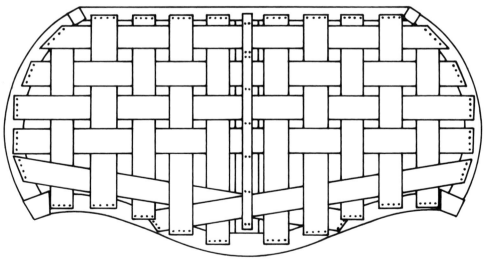

Sprung seats

Webs with springs sewn onto them should be a maximum of 2.5 cm (1 in) apart; closer than this is advisable rather than further apart.

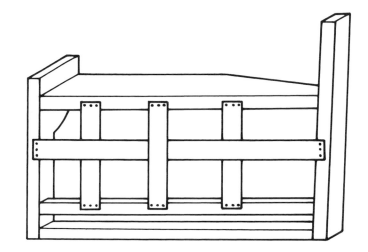

Arms

The spacing depends on the size of the arm. Two examples are given here. The number of webs used depends on the size of the open space between the rails.

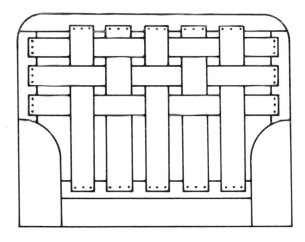

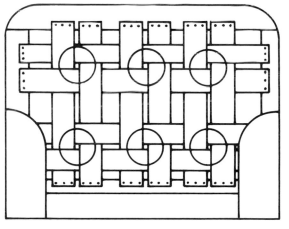

Back

This artwork shows webbing evenly spaced one web's distance apart covering the whole area of the back.

Here the webbing is placed in pairs to give maximum support to each spring.

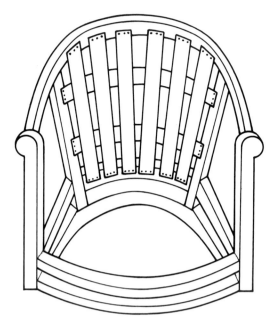

Tub chair

Shows how all the vertical webs have been applied in a fan shape, close together with the added support of two horizontal webs, which are not woven. This method of webbing offers maximum support, while at the same time maintaining the shape of the chair.

The measurements given here should only be used as a guide, as in some cases the shape of the frame can rule this impractical. For instance, if a chair is much wider at the front than the back, the webs may touch each other on the back rail and be up to 7.5 cm (3 in) apart on the front rail forming a fan layout.

When applying webbing to a back many layouts are possible. On a plain flat back the webbing may be placed up to 7.5 cm (3 in) apart whereas a tub chair will require the webbing to be no more than one web's distance apart, or 5 cm (2 in), at its widest point. This is because horizontal webs can rarely be fixed.

Whereas with a seat the webs should be placed a maximum of 2.5 cm (1 in) apart, allowances can be made when the webbing is fanned. Each spring is normally fixed to the webbing with a minimum of one horizontal and one vertical web behind it but two webs placed close together in each direction is recommended for a sprung back.

• **Accurate positioning**

It is also very important that the webs are placed accurately and that the distance between each web is equal where the frame permits. This will provide good support and assist in the positioning of springs, if used.

• **Using the correct tack and staple size**

It is important to use the correct tack and staple size when fixing webbing or hessian to a frame, especially if the frame has seen better days. Sometimes using a few more smaller-size tacks can be more appropriate for the frame you are working on and could result in less damage. In all cases you should fix the webbing with tacks in a staggered formation, using the U or W pattern of tack application, to help prevent splitting the frame rail. The U and W dictate the number of tacks used. This relates to the load that the webbing is required to support and the style and dimensions of the rail.

If using a pneumatic staple gun it is important to achieve a good coverage of staples to ensure a secure anchorage. I would recommend that on a 5-cm (2-in) width web, three lines of four 14 mm (⅝ in) staples are used.

MODERN WEBBING

Modern stretchable webbing, can be made either from natural latex, rubber or elastic which may include some natural rubber. Often, more than one type is used in combination to provide support and suspension. Rubber/elastic suspension is usually only found in the back or seat section of upholstered pieces and is sometimes only covered with a loose cushion or a layer of foam. In these cases the webbing provides the suspension and no springs are required.

Webs can be applied in a single direction only, either back to front (on a seat) or side to side (on a back), and the number of webs required is often dictated by the style and construction of the frame, but in all cases is governed by the manufacturer's guidelines as to the maximum distance apart the webs should be placed.

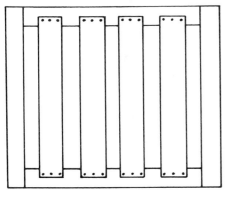

Single webbing layout

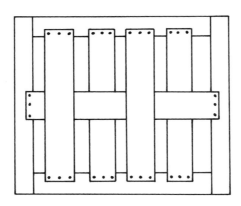

Preventing webs spreading

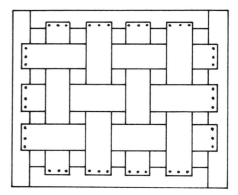

Total coverage

Webbing applied to a seat in a single direction only may force the webs to spread apart when sat on, which could result in the cushion placed over the webs to fall between them. This means that only the central area of the webbing is providing the support required.

Spreading can be prevented by adding side-to-side webbing. Note that the number of vertical and horizontal rubber or elasticated webs used here is not even: there are more webs applied back to front than side to side. The webs that run back to front are attached with no more than a web's width apart, while the woven side-to-side webs are spread much further apart to help prevent the webs spreading and to evenly distribute the load applied to the seat.

Webbing applied to a seat in both directions using a woven formation and using one or more webs will provide excellent support and an even distribution of load. Most manufacturers recommend the amount of stretch that needs to be applied when fixing webs to a frame, in order for the webbing to adequately support the load, but I have found this can vary. You will find that the longer the webbing the more it will stretch.

Elasticated webbing needs to be applied under slightly different conditions. Unlike rubber webbing, elasticated webbing is supplied in various strengths, which allows the upholsterer to choose the appropriate tension type for the purpose required (i.e. a seat or back of a chair) and to adapt the chair so that it can be produced with a firm or soft feel and/or support.

TIP: As a guide, after fixing the rubber webbing at one end and stretching it to fix it to the other end, you will notice that under tension the webbing appears to reduce slightly in width. As the web starts to narrow, and using this in combination with the manufacturer's guidelines, you will able to apply the webbing with universal tension throughout the area you are working on.

APPLYING HESSIAN

Hessian comes in a variety of weights and types, and each variety has its specific use. Hessian can be applied in two ways, either to a flat surface, such as a straight-edge top webbed dining seat, or to a shaped/domed surface, such as a sprung seat.

APPLYING HESSIAN TO A FLAT SURFACE

Cut a piece of 285 g (10 oz) hessian 5 cm (2 in) larger overall than the width and depth of the frame. Place the hessian over the frame, ensuring that you have equal amounts of hessian on all sides. Fold over the hessian by 2 cm (¾ in) at the front of the frame and permanently tack through the fold with a 10 mm (⅜ in) improved tack near the edge of the hessian, placing the tacks no more than 4 cm (1½ in) apart.

Starting in the middle at the back of the frame and working from the centre outwards, stretch the hessian taught, pulling directly away towards the rear of the frame from each tack applied to the front, and secure with a permanent tack. Continue until you have attached the hessian along the back rail. Now trim the hessian on one of the sides to allow a 2 cm (¾ in) fold and permanently tack the fold over as at the front. Now repeat to fix the sides of the frame by stretching, permanently tacking, folding and final fixing.

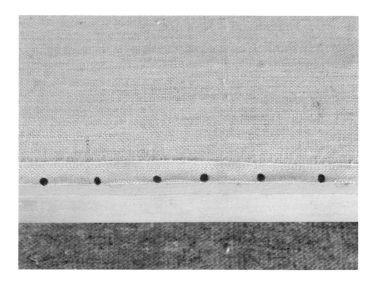

TIP: Aim to place the hessian along the centre of the rail, or if unable to do so, make sure the leading edge is kept clear. This will ensure that future construction will not be interfered with and that fillings will even out any unevenness that the hessian/webbing could cause. Remember to stop short of the corners, to allow central fixing of the hessian on the side rails.

TIP: Ensure the weave of the hessian is central and/or parallel to the frame. This is referred to as 'corridors'.

APPLYING HESSIAN TO A SHAPED/DOMED SURFACE

Hessian is also applied over a moulded shape, such as over springs. Ensure when choosing and measuring the hessian that you take into account the widest points of the surface and any allowance you require for shaping, then cut the hessian a minimum of 5 cm (2 in) larger all round than the measurement required.

Place the hessian over the frame/springs, ensuring that the corridors of the hessian are lined up to the frame and temporary tack the hessian where it lies over the highest points of the seat (i.e. the springs). This ensures the hessian can be correctly positioned and any fullness removed before finally tacking down.

Trim off all excess hessian, leaving a minimum 2 cm (¾ in) all round. Fold the hessian over and permanently tack down along the centre of the rail.

TIP: This type of covering over springs provides a platform for further fillings while at the same time allows the covering to flex and move with the seat springs. Therefore the tension required is not as it would be if placed over a non-suspension system, such as webbing.

SPRING AND SUSPENSION SYSTEMS

Spring and suspension systems used in upholstery come in all forms, ranging from steel through to reinforced rubber. The traditional type of springs that we know today first originated in the very early 1800s; prior to this, only various types of webbing were the used as the main support of any fixed upholstery. This chapter looks at a range of springs, most of which are still available today.

METAL SPRINGS

The basic material for making all metal springs is steel wire – the higher the carbon content, the more resistant and stiff the springs. Wire with a higher carbon content and good tensile strength is used to produce tension springs; standard spring steel wire is used for making cone-shaped and barrel springs used in mattress interiors. Springs used in upholstery are usually coated to prevent rusting. Cone springs, for instance, are coated with copper.

Double- and single-cone springs

Double-cone springs are also known as hourglass or waisted springs. Steel spring wires are produced in various gauges and sizes. The gauge is known as swg (standard wire gauge), the thickest being 8 swg down to very thin wires at 22 swg. Listed below are the various spring sizes and wire gauges for double- and single-cone springs. These springs are usually sold in bundles of 50 and 100.

HEIGHT	x	GAUGE
7.5 cm (3 in)	x	10 swg and 12 swg
10 cm (4 in)	x	9 swg, 10 swg and 12 swg
12.5 cm (5 in)	x	9 swg, 10 swg and 12 swg
15 cm (6 in)	x	9 swg, 10 swg and 12 swg
18 cm (7 in)	x	9 swg, 10 swg and 12 swg
20 cm (8 in)	x	8½ swg and 9 swg
23 cm (9 in)	x	8½ swg and 9 swg
25.5 cm (10 in)	x	8 swg and 9 swg
30.5 cm (12 in)	x	8 swg and 9 swg

Springs are manufactured on an automatic machine called a coiler and then knotted. The springs are produced at a rate of several hundreds per hour. The double-cone spring is reversible and knotted at both ends. The pitch of each coil is set by the coiling machine and varies in different springs. As the diameter of the coils becomes narrower, a firm area is produced at the centre of the spring. A single-cone spring is firmer at its base.

Tension or cable springs

Tension springs, also known as cable springs, are designed as a lateral suspension system and are stretched across the shortest distance in either a seat or back, usually from side to side. Due to their small diameter they take up very little space within the chair frame and are therefore ideal for lightweight wooden or metal frames. The springs are fixed under tension and are evenly spaced apart at a distance of 6.5 cm (2½ in). Two sizes are available for the upholstery industry: one for the seat and the other for the back. Seat springs are approximately 13 mm (½ in) in diameter and made of 18 swg while back springs are 7 mm (⁵⁄₁₆ in) in diameter and 14 swg. Both are available in lengths of up to 55 cm (21½ in).

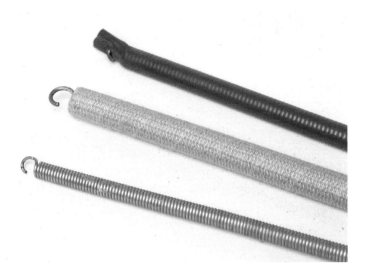

The seat springs usually only a have a loose cushion placed on them. When sat on these springs expand, opening the coils which could pinch and damage the fabric. To prevent this they are usually covered with a woven rayon sock, or in the case of modern springs, a plastic sleeve. The back springs are not usually covered, as a protective layer of hessian or similar material will be used over the springs prior to applying the filling.

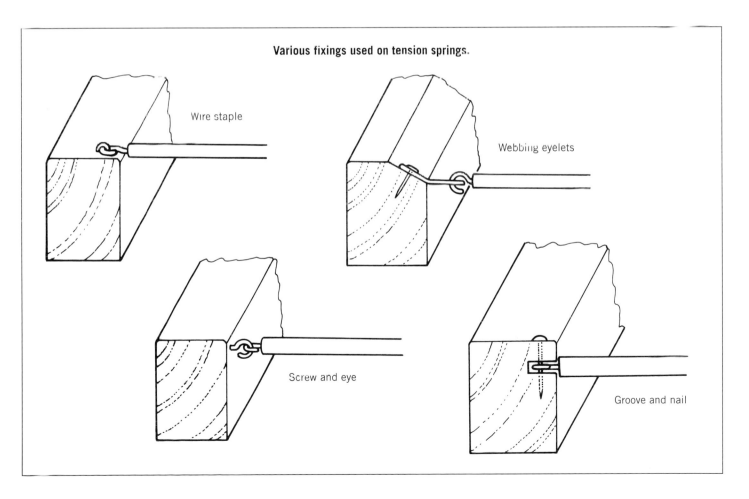

Various fixings used on tension springs.

Wire staple

Webbing eyelets

Screw and eye

Groove and nail

Spring units

Single-cone springs are not available individually and are made specifically for use in spring units. They are riveted onto steel laths and covered with a mesh stop. They are also used in bed bases and supported on metal U bars. A spring unit is made up of a number of springs assembled and linked together. The units are factory-made and supplied ready for use in upholstery and the manufacture of bedding. There are several different types, reversible and non-reversible, made up from compression and tension springs. Generally, reversible units are used for mattresses and cushions. The non-reversible units are fixed into seating with laths and wires.

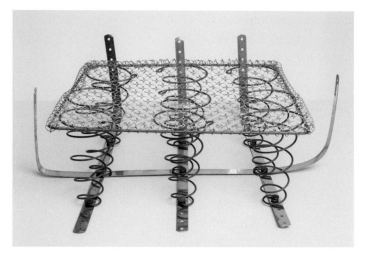

Barrel and pocket springs

Barrel springs are made from finer gauge wires. They are straight-sided and are designed for use in mattress-making. Although much softer to feel and lighter in weight, they are grouped closer together into pocket spring units. As many as 1,800 springs may be used in a modern double mattress. Each spring is pocketed in cotton calico, separated by a sewn seam and the single rows of pocketed springs are clipped together to form a larger mattress unit. The unit is completed with a metal edge strip or wire clipped to the outer springs.

Serpentine or zigzag springs

These are tension-type springs of a completely different wire formation. Unlike tension springs, serpentine springs are usually fixed front to back and up and down. High-carbon steel wire is formed into a sinuous strip of various widths and from different wire gauge sizes. As the serpentine spring is produced, the continuous strips may be arched, semi-arched or flat formed. The machines that make them can be set to produce continuous 30 m (100 ft) rolls, or cut lengths in batches or nests of any number.

The ends of cut strips are kinked to provide a non-slip fixing in the clip. A hooked end can also be formed where springs are to be directly located into holes in metal chair frames. The standard wire gauges used for serpentine springs generally range from 9 to 12 swg: 9 and 10 swg for seat springs, and 11 and 12 swg for back springs. These are available in widths of approximately 5–7.5 cm (2–3 in), of which the 5 cm (2 in) widths are the most

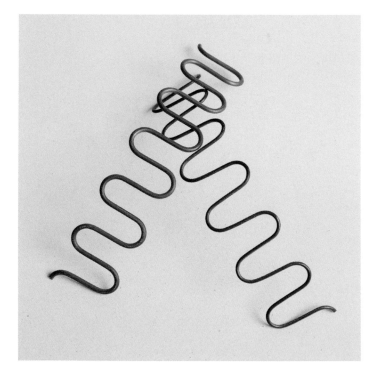

common. By nature, the high-carbon wire used for the springs is very tough and can only be cut with heavy bolt croppers or a bench-mounted cutter designed especially for wire cutting.

Positioning serpentine springs

The positioning of serpentine springs is very important. Based on a 5-cm (2-in) spring, the centre point of each spring clip should be placed no more than 10 cm (4 in) apart. This distance can of course be reduced but should never be increased. For instance, on a shaped frame which is wider at the front than at the back the springs will be fixed at a distance of 10 cm (4 in) on the front rail and 9 cm (3½ in) on the back rail.

Measuring and cutting serpentine springs

Prior to cutting the springs, consideration should be given to the shape you are trying to achieve. Whether you wish to form a flat surface, a slightly domed finish or a curved shape, the blue clips that hold the springs should be fixed into position. This will allow you to apply a single spring to check for the correct tension and shape. To work out the length of spring required for a flat surface, measure the gap between the clips. This measurement will be the minimum length required for a flat seat. Always cut the spring slightly oversize and never undersize; you can trim the spring to length once you are satisfied with the overall shape. To form a dome shape, one or more additional spring 'loops' may be

required. For a more pronounced curve, further additional spring loops will be needed. In all cases the use of a steel tape will give you the approximate measurement required but it is a case of trial and error to achieve the shape you require.

RUBBER AND ELASTICATED WEBBING

On some occasions webbing can be used as a form of suspension system as some seats don't always need filling and a cushion is placed directly over the webs instead. As described in Upholstery sundries (see pages 14–15), webbing is made up of natural and/or a mixture of both natural and synthetic materials. Various fixings are available to attach both types of webbing, the easiest to use being tacks and staples. These fixings are usually used when the webbing is not exposed. Others fixings available are the metal plate for wooden rails that have been grooved out to accept the plate fixing, and the A clip, used in conjunction with a plate and staple for metal frames.

APPLYING SPRINGS AND SPRING UNITS

For nearly two hundred years upholsterers have used a variety of springs to provide support and comfort to upholstered furniture. The double-cone or hourglass spring was first patented and standardised in 1828 by Samuel Pratt. Since then there have been several variations of this spring, resulting in the single-cone spring, which comes in a variety of shapes, sizes and gauges and is used in pre-assembled spring units. The application and fixing of these two types of spring can be categorised either under the headings of traditional or modern.

TRADITIONAL SPRINGS

When applying these springs you will need to decide both the height and gauge of the springs required for the type of construction you are undertaking (i.e. seat, back or arm) and the type/style of finish required to that part of the chair. You must also consider the positioning of the springs, especially in backs and seats. Because of the shape of the chair, it is not always possible to apply the springs in a symmetrical pattern, using an equal number of springs in both directions, as shown in the diagrams.

When positioning the springs ensure you use enough to maintain the correct support for the item you are working on, but be careful not to overload the area, which would lead to the springs interfering with each other or with the frame around the edge of the sprung area. This could

**Examples of spring layouts and how the springs
will be lashed after fixing.**

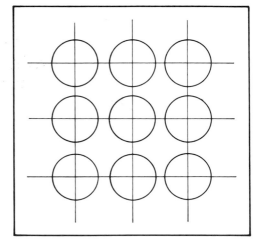
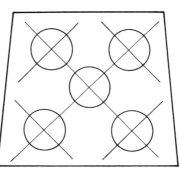
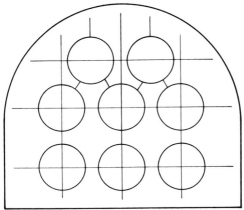

result in poor operation and/or the springs knocking against each other as they compress. I would recommend positioning the springs about 2.5 cm (1 in) apart. When placing the springs, look at the bottom ring on the webbing – some springs, whether they are new or old, do not always sit perfectly upright until they are set and secured at the top.

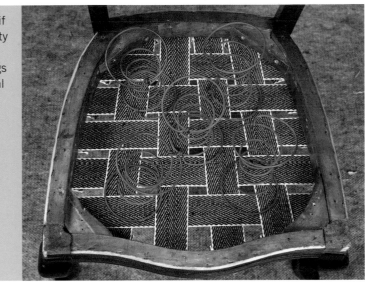

TIP: Remember, if you have difficulty deciding the number of springs required it is vital that the central area of any construction is fully supported by springs, as it will bear most of the weight.

Attaching traditional springs to webbing
In most cases, traditional springs are attached to webbing with twine, with each spring sewn to the webbing at four equally spaced points around the bottom ring. This can be done using a large curved or spring needle and four-cord twine. Thread the twine through the webbing from the underside against one side of the spring wire. Pass it over the wire and back through the webbing to the underside of the webbing, then make a slip knot. Pass the same length of twine through the web again, forming a loop over the spring and a simple knot on the underside. Continue to apply four knots per spring until all the springs are attached or you run out of twine. If this is the case make a double knot to ensure the twine cannot undo. On large areas you will use several lengths of twine to sew in all your springs.

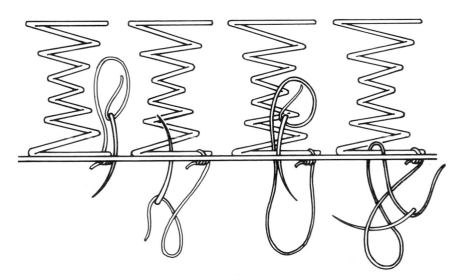

Lashing the springs

The term 'lashing' describes the method used to stabilise double-cone springs. Lashing cord, more commonly known as laid cord, controls the direction in which the springs compress. Lashing allows the springs to compress following their cylindrical shape and when the compression is removed they return to their original height and tied position. If a spring is only lashed in one direction or no lashing is used, it will very quickly buckle or snap, leaving sharp metal ends, which could pierce the upholstery filling and cause injury.

To attach the lashing, anchor the laid cord to the rail furthest from you, normally using a 16 mm (⅝ in) improved tack. Stretch the cord across the line of springs and position the furthest spring so that it is leaning slightly towards the tack beneath the cord. While holding the spring in position knot the cord around it using a clove hitch knot. Tie the cord to the opposite side of the spring and repeat the process across the whole line. The central springs should always be lashed in an upright position while the edge springs should lean towards the frame. Complete the line by twisting the cord around the tack nearest to you and hammer it down to secure the cord in place.

The lashing is attached to form two types of finish. A domed/full seat finish allows the upholsterer to lash the springs so that the outer springs lie out towards the edge of the frame and are slightly compressed at the outer edge to form a dome.

A cushion finish allows the upholsterer to keep the outer springs in a more upright finish, forming a platform for the cushion to sit on.

This drawing shows how 18 cm (7 in) or taller springs should be double or middle lashed. This type of lashing is necessary due to the height of the spring, which would in time buckle at its centre, if not lashed.

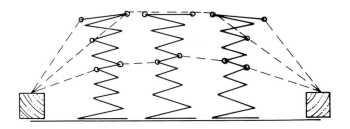

Modern spring units

For over 50 years the spring unit has aided the upholsterer in providing comfort and longevity to the life of upholstered furniture. It has many advantages: made entirely of metal, the spring unit does not naturally deteriorate as webbing does. It can be formed into almost any shape and size, allowing greater flexibility in the design of the seat or back of a chair. The unit is constructed in such a manner that once it is fixed to the frame a few simple lashings applied in appropriate places control all necessary movement. Finally, both modern and traditional fillings may be used to provide the final shape and comfort.

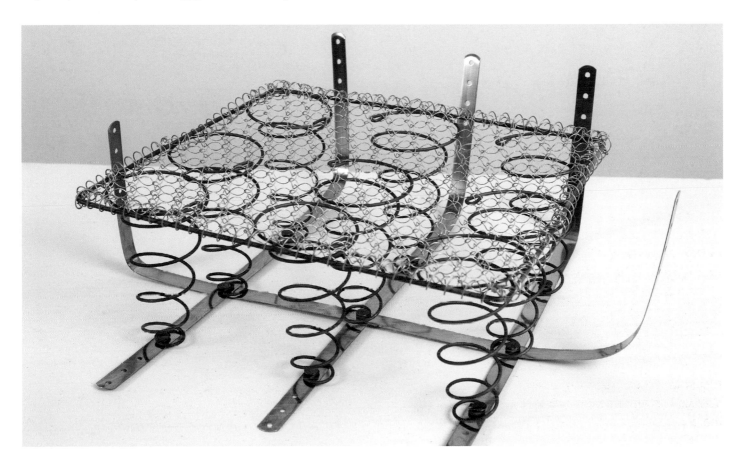

Applying spring units

To apply a spring unit, mark the centre of both the front and back rails. This will allow you to set the unit in the correct position. Slide the unit into the frame, allowing the back laths (metal webs) to pass through over the seat rail at the back of the frame. If the unit has side laths these are usually bent into the spring to pass by the front post of the arm. When the spring unit is in position within the frame, any side laths can now be straightened and passed through the side of the frame.

TIP: Check for any protruding wire ends along the top edge of the spring that could damage the upholstery you have already applied as you slide the unit in. If you are working with light coloured material, then cover the spring as some units have a very thin layer of oil applied to prevent rusting until used.

Bend back the side laths so they are ready to be attached. Starting at the front with the middle lath, position the unit and hammer a 2.5 cm (1 in) clout nail through the hole provided and continue to do this on all the laths along the front rail, ensuring that each lath is positioned correctly in line with the middle lath.

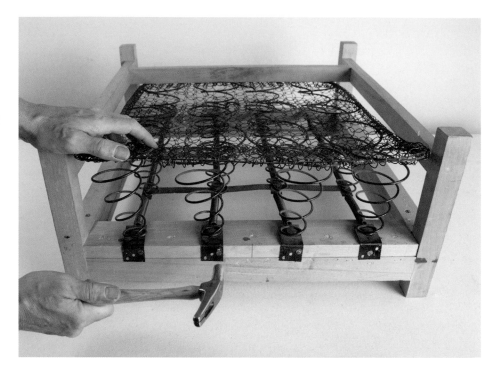

Stand at the back of the chair in preparation to stretch and attach the rear laths. If you do not have a lath stretcher to stretch the laths, then a pair of pincers will provide sufficient grip. Stretch the laths so that they are pulled out straight and hammer a clout nail in each hole provided. After all the laths are attached bend the laths around the side of the seat rails and apply another clout nail on the side to ensure a secure fixing.

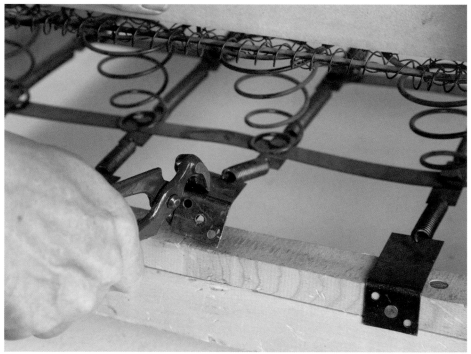

TIP: You may be required to add additional holes to the laths of the spring unit, as the holes provided will on occasion not match up to the frame. You can do this using either a drill or a punch.

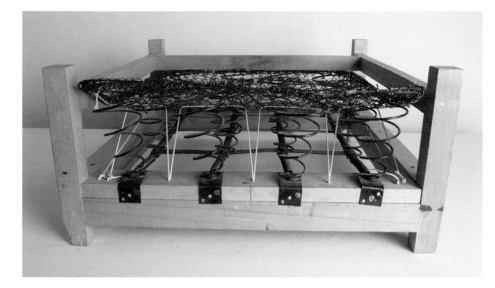

The unit will have some movement from back to front that will require a measure of control. To control this movement while at the same time allowing the springs to operate properly, you will need to lash the springs as shown here. In most pieces of furniture the arms will prevent side movement but if necessary side lashings should be applied in a similar fashion to prevent sideways movement.

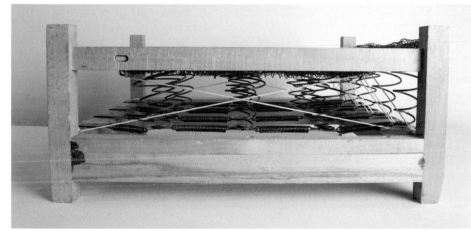

The lashings across the front of the springs are only required when using a cushion on top of the spring unit. These lashings help to form a seat lip, which will prevent the cushion from slipping forward off the seat.

The springs should then be covered with (340 g) 12 oz hessian, which is tacked/stapled to the seat rail and stitched along the edge wire using a blanket stitch to prevent wear to the hessian. The unit may now be covered using either modern or traditional fillings and materials.

CUTTING AROUND FRAMES

Cutting fabric around frames is probably one of the most challenging aspects of upholstery, especially when you are required to either wrap the fabric around a post or to change the direction of the fabric. When starting out, it can be difficult to visualise the cuts you are required to make, with the added difficulty that most cuts are made while the fabric is folded back in a mirrored position. If care is not taken, the opposite angle to that which is required can end up being cut! The series of drawings in this chapter will help you understand what is required. As with all operations in upholstery, be prepared to make technical variations in how you make your cuts to achieve the required outcome.

TIP: If you are unsure of any cuts, one of the easiest ways of practising is to place a piece of scrap fabric, such as calico, over the fabric that you have fixed in place. You can cut into the calico, then unfold and lay out around the area that you are working on. If any errors are made, these can be corrected when you cut the top fabric.

Remember! Always undercut and test for the correct positioning and length of the cut. You can always extend cuts but you can never undo a cut.

V AND Y CUTS

Here, an equal amount of fabric appears on both sides of the rail. This is usually done so that an equal amount of fabric can be folded in to form a pleat. The straight cut, identified as A, is a single incision made to allow close access to the frame prior to forming the V cut. This should not be confused with the Y cut, which in many cases may not be required.

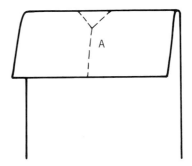

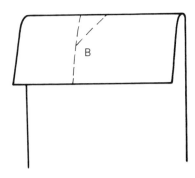

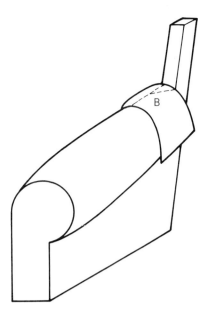

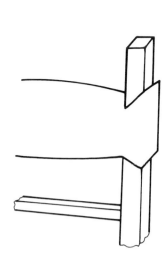

The Y cut can be looked upon as a specialised cut, inasmuch as it is deliberately cut so that an excess amount of fabric is placed on one side.

The first cut, B, is made on the inside of the arm. This releases tension in the fabric and allows you to check that the fabric is in the correct position; should it not be, you have the width of the post to move it to the outside. Alternatively, if you need to move the fabric to the inside you could apply a second parallel straight cut; in either case the second part of the Y would be cut.

One of the main reasons for a Y cut is to allow maximum cover of the outside edge of the post, which allows future layers of fabric, such as those used on the inside back, to be folded over the arm fabric, ensuring that no part of the frame will be exposed throughout its lifespan.

THE CORNER CUT

Here, a simple diagonal cut allows equal amounts of fabric, which will be formed into pleats, to pass down each side of the leg/post.

Here the cut has been started at the corner point. You should ensure that when positioning the fabric prior to cutting it is lying at the correct angle to the corner, then cut it at 45 degree angle. In nearly all cases the starting point of the cut will be offset to the corner of the fabric.

TIP: Always ensure the fabric is correctly tensioned and temporary tacked into position; you can partly release the fabric for cutting either one corner or one side, but you must always re-fix the fabric into position as you complete each cut. This will prevent the movement of fabric or accidentally exposing a mirrored cut, such as at the back of a dining chair, which should have been secured into position prior to making a second cut.

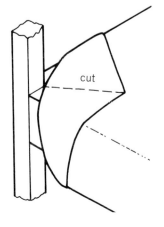

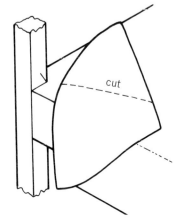

ROUND OR 'OFFSET' CORNERS

This drawing shows the cuts required to allow the fabric to pass between the back legs/posts. This method of cutting should be carried out with great care and accuracy to provide you with sufficient fabric to form pleats on both sides of the leg/post. It is a form of Y cut. Note that the first cuts on the outer edges are at a slight outward angle to provide you with the additional material needed for the pleats.

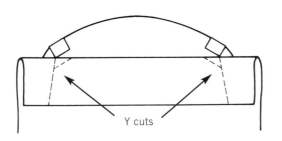

Y cuts

LEG/SHOW WOOD CUTS

To cut around show wood legs or similar, ensure that the fabric is under tension in the required position over one of the legs and cut diagonally across the show wood. This will provide you with sufficient fabric to form a pleat both across the leg and on the underside of the frame, which will give a very neat finish as well as preventing the fabric from fraying or leaving exposed cut edges.

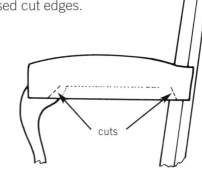

cuts

CUTTING AROUND A WING

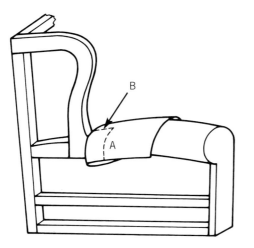

B

A

This side view of a wing chair shows the arm fabric having been released from the back and folded back on itself in preparation for cutting. The front, top and bottom of the fabric remain securely fixed in place so that the fabric cannot move. If the bottom of the wing upright is 7.5 cm (3 in) wide, the vertical cut, A, is made 5 cm (2 in) from the fold. When the cut is parallel to the centre of the wing, a right-angled cut is made; fold the 5 cm (2 in) flap back and tack to the outside of the wing (B).

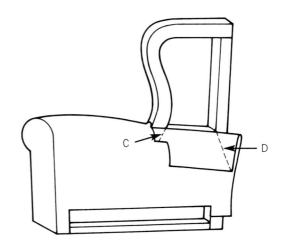

C

D

This drawing shows the fabric that you have just cut and released from the inside view of the arm. Apply tension towards the back and fix. Make a V cut, as shown at cut C. The final cut, D, will allow the flap of fabric to pass through the wing and be fixed, maintaining on completion a fixing throughout the top length of the arm and maximum cover to the upholstered frame.

MANIPULATING LININGS AND FABRICS

This chapter will guide you in the application of various types of covering. In most examples described, I refer to the use of scrim, striped or symmetrically patterned materials. Following a simple formula of application, both of setting the material (temporary tacking) and permanently fixing it, will ensure the fabric/covering is correctly set in relation to shape, height and pattern.

APPLYING COVERING MATERIALS

Straight edges

When working on a rectangular frame, such as that of a stool for example, you should ensure the scrim is set squarely on the frame when applying it in preparation for stitching.

You can then tack down the scrim following a horizontal thread in the scrim along the bevelled edge you have prepared prior to any upholstery being applied. This will ensure that the height and any overhang required remain constant, which will help create a crisp and accurate finish to the edge.

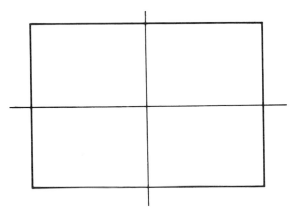

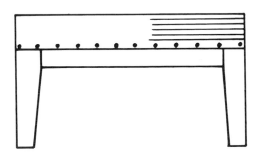

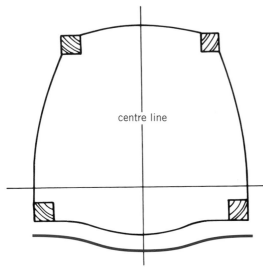

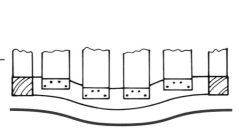

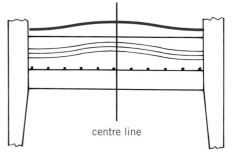

Shaped or scalloped edges

When working with frames that are partly or fully shaped, the method of setting the scrim or fabric remains the same. Using the guide lines shown here, lay the scrim/fabric centrally over the area of the chair, and using temporary tacks, fix the material so that the weave of the material matches the lines. This will ensure that the material is correctly positioned.

Before tacking down the scrim to the bevelled edge, look at the underside of the frame and note, in this case, the shape of the front rail.

By following the shape of the front rail and applying this shape to a single horizontal thread of the scrim you will be able to tack down the scrim and form almost the exact shape of the front edge. Note that from any equal measurement from the centre line outwards, the position of the horizontal thread mirrors that of the frame. This will ensure that the height of the edge and any overhang remains constant.

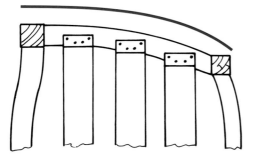

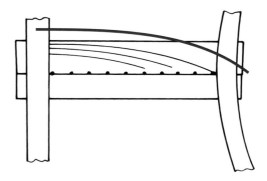

A second example of this method of following the shape of a rail is by examining the side curved rail of the same frame. Look at the underside of the frame and note the shape of the side rail.

When applying the scrim in this case, the horizontal thread of the scrim curves downwards towards the back of the frame, forming the required shape. If the side rail has no shape and is at an angle of more or less than 90 degrees to the front rail, then the horizontal thread of the scrim will follow an upwards or downwards line in relation to the frame. This method can be applied to almost any shape you require when constructing either a back or seat.

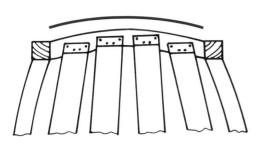

The diagram on the left shows the curved shape of the rail from the underside of the frame. On the right, the threads of the scrim are tacked down to follow the shape of the frame and are mirrored on either side of the centre. This method can be applied to any part of the upholstered item where there is an equal curve.

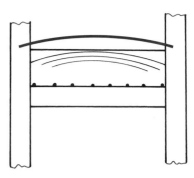

Scroll or similar shaped arms

The method of applying covering materials to scroll arms is slightly different to the one used for seats and backs, inasmuch as arms have corridors rather than central lines. With seats and backs there is always a central line/feature from front to back and if not central, a parallel line/feature running side to side.

CORRIDORS The term 'corridor' is often used to describe a specific section of a panel, whether it be hessian or top fabric. A corridor is an invisible narrow band within a fabric panel that runs both vertically and horizontally, enabling the fabric to be correctly positioned to give the impression that it is set square. Using corridors in this way is especially important when positioning striped or patterned fabrics as it ensures the stripes or pattern run straight.

The vertical central line in an arm is at the front, while the horizontal line runs centrally across the top of the arm. The method of application shown here ensures that the arm can be constructed in a balanced way, resulting in an even distribution of excess covering material on both sides of the arm, as most arms will reduce in size/diameter towards the rear. When this method is applied it will assist in completing the tacking off of the rear, top and bottom of the arm.

With regard to the front of a scroll arm it is important that the threads that come over the top of the stuffing follow the shape of the arm. The threads should not be distorted as this would result in very poor finishing; the scrim may have to be gathered or pleated in order to achieve the required shape.

Think of the front of the round shape at the top of the scroll arm as a cartwheel, with each thread that comes round the front as a spoke in the wheel. The thread should, in every case, aim for the centre of the arm to ensure that the covering material, with a small amount of gathering/pleating between each fixing, is evenly distributed around the edge of the frame.

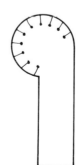

APPLYING TOP FABRICS

Up until now I have referred to the positioning of construction covering materials, such as hessians, scrims and linings, to form some of the most basic forms of construction, the principles of which can be applied to nearly all types of upholstery construction. The following information is a guide to applying top fabric, especially patterned fabric.

When applying top fabric every effort should be made to ensure that it is to your or your customer's total satisfaction, that the cover is applied

correctly and that it appears straight to the eye. With a rectangular shape, such as the seat of a stool, the dome of the seat must be taken into account: the pattern may develop a slight curve on the sides of the stool, giving the appearance that the pattern will drop at the corners.

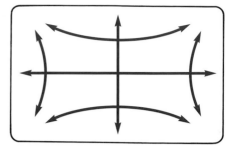

The directional lines here show how the fabric would form on a domed seat. With the carver chair, not only does the dome effect apply but the shape of the chair intensifies the distortion of the fabric as the cover is wrapped over the front. The pattern should be even and balanced, while at the sides the fabric will drop down, towards the back of the frame.

Striped patterns

Covering arms can raise a variety of issues when using striped or symmetrical patterns. Usually the pattern should be positioned using the corridors and the cartwheel positioning for the pleats that come over the front of the arm.

In the case of stripes, it may be necessary to move the vertical corridor slightly to the rear of the arm to give the impression that all or most of the stripes are vertical. The diagrams show the two types of application of plain or basic patterned fabric and striped fabric. Note how, with the use of the arrows, the flow of the pattern can vary.

TIP: The finished appearance of a fabric on a chair should always look vertical/horizontal on each separate area and centralised to the eye, but if measured this will not always be the case. Upholstery is the most inaccurate form of construction within the furniture industry but the unique skill of the craftsman makes it appear easy!

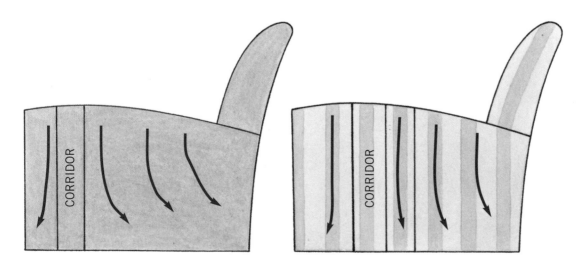

CORNER PLEATS

In the completion stages of an upholstered chair there is a good chance that you will be required to make one or more pleats to allow the fabric to mould around the shape that has been constructed. The stages below will guide you in the construction of single and double pleats. In all cases, pleats are only formed at the very final stage of fabric application.

SINGLE CORNER PLEATS

The single pleat is used when folding scrim or top fabric to form a square corner which needs to look both neat and sharp.

1 Start by tacking the first side up to and around the corner. If there is an indent when rounding the corner, apply more filling so that the corner is properly formed.

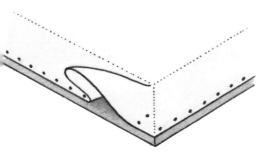

2 Fold the fabric to form a pleat. This will identify the surplus fabric that you need to cut away.

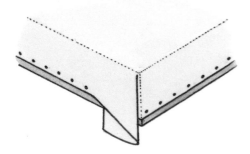

3 While holding the pleat, lift up the fabric and cut away the excess material, making sure you only cut up to the tack and are careful not to cut too much fabric away.

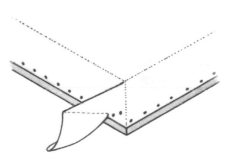

4 Now re-fold the fabric to form a neat finish, ensuring that the fabric under the fold is folded flat. It is advisable for the pleat to be fixed fractionally just short of the corner – if the pleat is placed at the very edge of the corner it may appear to 'fall' round the corner.

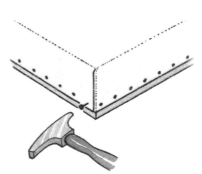

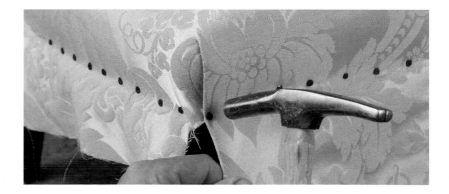

DOUBLE CORNER PLEATS

The double pleat, also known as the Price of Wales pleat, is usually applied to soft or rounded corners, where a single pleat would look untidy or as though it had been placed in the wrong position. This type of pleat provides a very neat finish to rounded corners. To achieve the double pleat follow these steps:

1 Pull the material down, making sure that there is an equal amount of fabric on both sides of the corner. Place a single temporary tack in the centre, then place two permanent tacks on either side of the corner; the temporary tack will provide an anchorage point and keep the fabric under tension while you apply the permanent tacks.

2 Cut away the excess fabric to prevent a build up of bulky material under the pleats if a thick top fabric is being used.

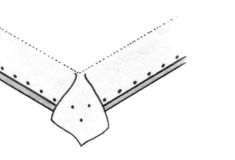

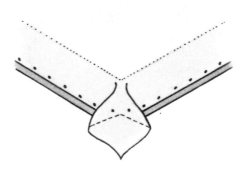

3 Now fold each pleat and fix separately in place. Note that the pleats lie at an angle and do not come into contact with each other at the point where they are tacked.

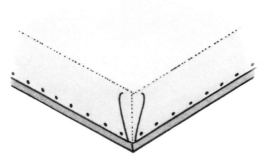

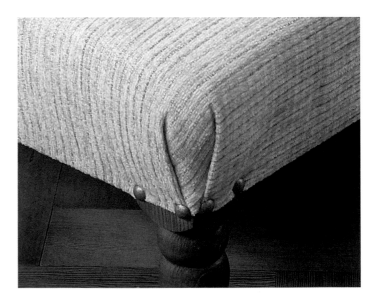

KNUTS AND STITCHES

Here you will see various knots and stitches, how they are formed and where they are used.
It is important that these knots and stitches are formed and attached both correctly and securely
in order that they operate in the intended manner throughout the life of the upholstered piece.

SLIP KNOT

The 'slipknot', sometimes known as the upholsterer's knot, is probably the most commonly used knot in upholstery. It is used when starting most forms of stitching, anchoring buttons and is the first knot used for tying down springs. The illustrations show how the slip knot is constructed and finally tied off. It should be noted that many upholsterers vary the way they form this knot, but all end up with the same secure fixing.

BLANKET STITCH

This stitch is used when sewing a corner pleat together that is not visible in a completed chair. It is simply passed through all the folds of the corner and starting with a slip knot followed by a single knot binds the pleat together.

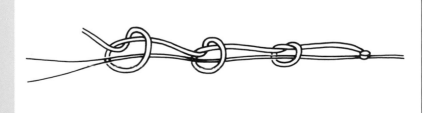

BLIND STITCH

The blind stitch is used for the purpose of firming up and forming the shape of the seat edge. The needle is passed through the front and top of the scrim at approximately a 45 degree angle until the eye of the needle is exposed, the needle is then returned at a slight angle so as to exit the front of the edge approximately 2.5 cm (1 in) to the left of the original entry. This forms a loop of twine within the stuffing. A slip knot should then be applied, then wrap the cord around your right hand and 'snatch' it towards the right of the stitch, while pinching the edge with your left hand in order to tighten the loop that you have formed and draw the first stuffing towards the front edge.

The second and all future stitches should be inserted in a similar fashion. To knot off a stitch, leave the needle protruding out of the exit hole and wind the cord that is connected to the previous stitch clockwise three times around the needle, pull the needle out of the edge and pull the cord tight as with the slip knot.

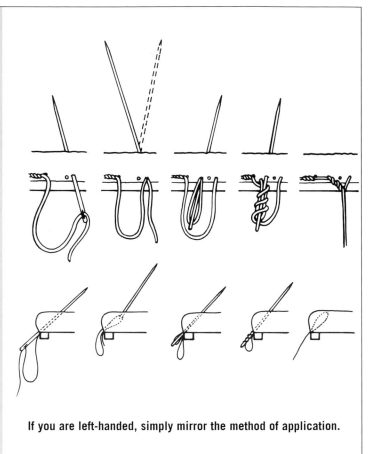

If you are left-handed, simply mirror the method of application.

TOP OR ROLL STITCH

The application of the top or roll stitch is identical to the blind stitch, with one exception. Instead of returning the needle on sight of the eye, it is lifted out of the scrim and moved to the left approximately 2.5 cm (1 in) where it re-enters the scrim, after which the same knotting process is applied as the blind stitch.

In deciding how many blind or top stitches are required, it is recommended that a space of no more than 1.5 cm (⅝ in) between each line of stitches should be applied. The number of stitches is always dictated by the height, shape and style of the finished piece.

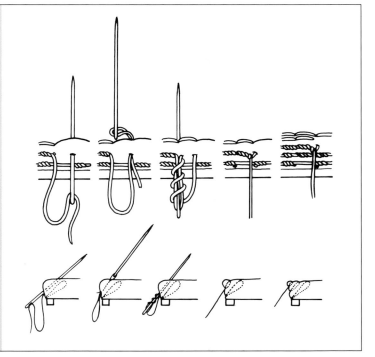

LOCK LOOP AND CLOVE HITCH KNOT

Two types of knot are generally used for lashing springs and spring systems. Fig 1 shows a lock loop, sometimes known as a half hitch knot. Fig 2 is a clove hitch knot, which is easy to apply and very secure, while at the same time can be easily loosened for adjustment when applying the laid cord to the springs.

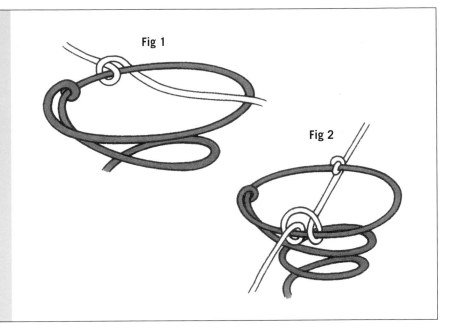

Fig 1

Fig 2

SLIP OR CASTLE STITCH

In the final stages of the application of the outside fabrics and for closing off cushions you are often required to slip stitch two or more pieces of fabric together. Start by securing the slipping thread. This can be done in a variety of ways such as using a slip knot or tacking the thread to the frame. Then using a small curved needle, pass the needle so that you catch approximately 1 cm (¾ in) of the fabric, then following the same process, pass the needle through the fabric that you wish to connect to starting directly opposite the exit hole of the previous stitch. Continue to do this for two or three stitches, then pull the thread tight so as to draw the two covers together. Continue to do this until you have completed the stitching and secure the thread in an appropriate manner.

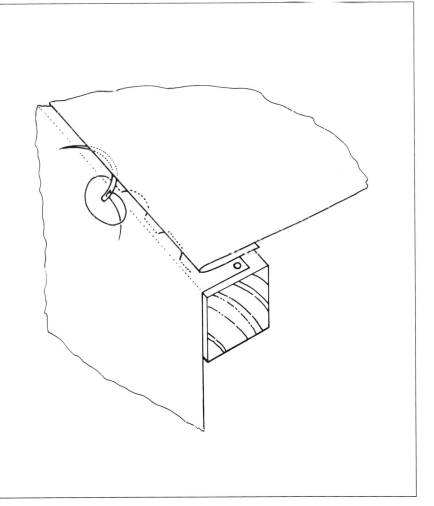

TRIMMINGS

There have been many styles of furniture design over the centuries, many of which have required some form of trimming. Trimmings are used to cover tacks along a decorative show-wood edge or are added purely to enhance a piece of furniture. Trimmings come under five categories: fringes, ruches, cords, braids and decorative nails, and within these categories are various designs, all of which are fixed in a variety of ways.

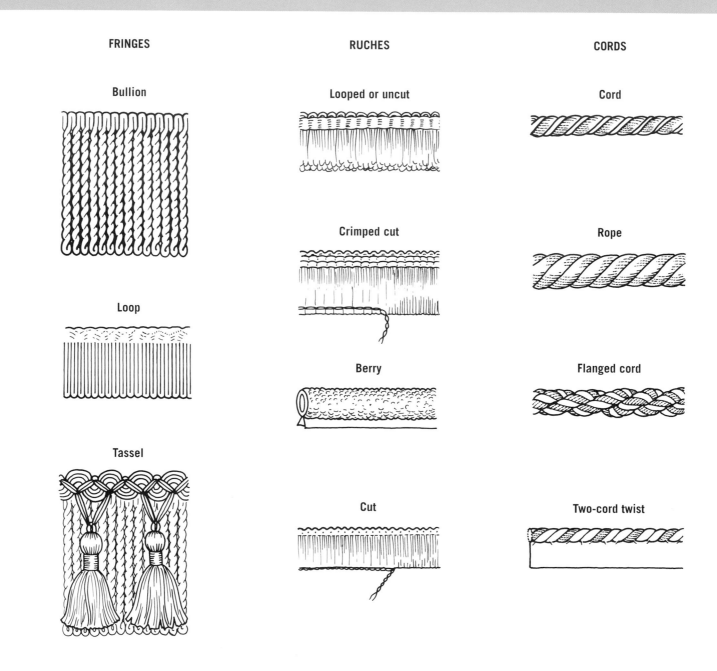

FRINGES

Bullion

Loop

Tassel

RUCHES

Looped or uncut

Crimped cut

Berry

Cut

CORDS

Cord

Rope

Flanged cord

Two-cord twist

BRAIDS

Scroll gimp

Coronation gimp

Argyle gimp

Oxford gimp

Border gimp

TRIMMINGS	STYLES	METHOD OF ATTACHMENT
Fringes	Bullion Loop Tassel	Hand-sewn Glued Fixed with decorative nails
Ruches	Looped or uncut Crimped cut Berry Cut	Usually incorporated in the sewing machine process but can be tacked to a frame
Cords	Cord Rope Two-cord twist Flanged cord	Hand-sewn or glued Hand-sewn or machined
Braids	Scroll gimp Coronation gimp Argyle gimp Oxford gimp Border gimp	Glued Fixed with gimp pins
Decorative nails	Dome-headed names in various finishes, including copper and nickel Pattern-headed nails, both round and square Enamel-headed nails in various colours	Hammered into position. Some upholsterers use a nylon-tipped hammer

Stuffed and stitched dining chair

Victorian nursing chair

Modern deep-buttoned stool

PROJECTS

Modern headboard

Child's chair

Boxed or border cushion

Day bed

STUFFED AND STITCHED DINING CHAIR

The dining room chair has been around for several centuries and comes in a variety of forms, ranging from a simple plain wooden frame with no padding, through to the highly involved traditional construction, and the modern foam seat. This project will introduce you to the type of traditional construction that upholsterers have used for over two hundred years.

Tools

- Upholstery hammer
- Upholstery scissors
- Wooden mallet
- Ripping chisel
- Web strainer
- Upholstery shears
- Tack lifter
- Pincers
- Craft knife
- Trimming knife
- Rasp

Needle kit

- Regulator
- Double-ended bayonet needle
- Spring needles
- Semi-circular slipping needles
- Upholstery skewers
- Upholstery pins
- Tape measure and metre rule
- Tailor's chalk

Sundries and fillings

- Webbing
- Hessians
- Scrim
- Fibre
- Hair
- Calico
- Skin wadding
- Various grades and sizes of tacks
- Top fabric
- Bottoming cloth
- 4-cord or nylon twine
- Decorative braid
- Glue for braid

■ In most cases you will be starting with an old piece of furniture, which will require the removal of all the upholstery materials. This must be done with some care and consideration to both the frame and your own safety. If you are attempting this or any other project for the first time, I would recommend that you remove the various layers of materials one at a time to understand the make-up of the order in which they are applied, as well as the type of materials used.

Ripping down

If you are using an old frame you will need to remove the bottom cloth, then each layer of material. See pages 42–44 for further instructions.

Frame preparation

1 & 2 Old furniture that has been upholstered several times will more often than not require minor repairs. One of the two most common problems being a joint in the frame that has dried out and become loose. This can easily be rectified by spreading the joint to allow the application of wood glue to the joint, which would then need re-clamping and should be left to dry preferably over several hours before starting any upholstery.

3 The second most common problem is the high number of tack holes in the frame due to it having been re-upholstered several times. On condition the rails are still sound, these can easily be filled by mixing saw dust – preferably the type you would get from an electrical sander – with a modern PVA wood glue. The texture of the mixture should be that of toothpaste to allow easy application. The paste can be applied either with a spreader or using your fingers, but be careful of any splinters or sharp objects. The advantage of using your fingers is that you can feel the holes and ensure a full and proper application of the filling.

4 After application, smooth over with a damp sponge, dry with a soft cloth and sand down with medium glass paper to remove the rough surface. Finally re-bevel the upper outer edge of the frame.

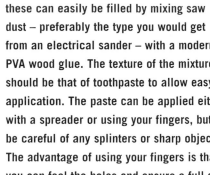

Webbing

5 Webbing should be applied on the upper side of the frame using 4 x 3 number of webs and 13 mm (½ in) improved tacks. To apply the webbing fix one end of the folded web and using the web strainer stretch and fix the other end to the frame (for further details see pages 45–49).

TIP: Remember the webs should be stretched to form a support strong enough to take a person's body weight but not so stretched that they will twist or break the chair frame/rails or tear the webbing away from the tacks.

TIP: Pad the end of the web strainer to prevent damage to the polished wood.

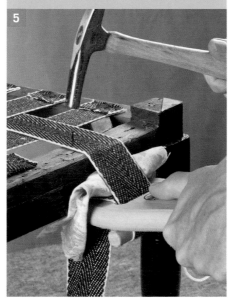

6 Note the position of the webs: the folded ends stop short of the outer edge of the frame. This is so that they do not interfere with a later stage of the construction – having the edge of the frame clear will provide you with a clean line for when the calico and top fabric are applied.

Hessian

7 You now require a piece of 285 g (10 oz) hessian to cover the webbing. Cut this approximately 5 cm (2 in) larger than the frame and apply with 10 mm (⅜ in) improved tacks (see pages 50–51). Again ensure you leave the outer edge of the frame clear for the later stages of construction. The corners of the hessian can either be folded diagonally and pleated across the corner, then tacked into position, or if the frame demands it, cut at a 45 degree angle and folded around the frame (see techniques, pages 62–63).

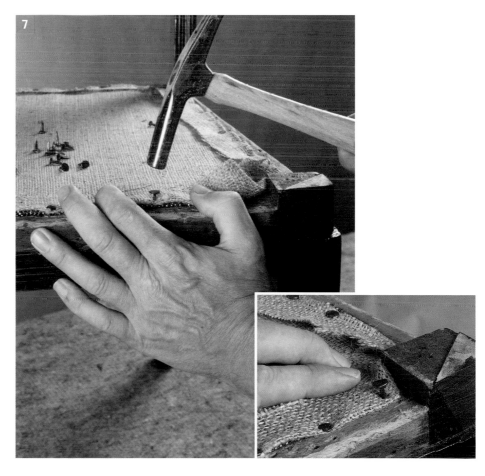

Bridal ties

8 Now apply the bridal ties to secure the stuffing. These ties are the starting process that allows you to place and hold in position the first filling but will help to control and maintain the positioning of the fibre throughout the seat's life. Note how the ties are laid out to give maximum coverage and support. Nylon twine instead of natural twine has been used here for the purpose of photography as it is lighter in colour and shows up more clearly against the hessian.

First stuffing

9 It is now time to apply the fibre that will form the support, shape and comfort of the seat. Take a reasonably large handful of fibre and tease it well to ensure that there are no clumps or balls of fibre and it is loose in texture and feels even throughout. Apply the first handful by scooping in an under-hand method under the loops of twine, ensuring that you do not ball or compact the fibre at the tips of you fingers as you apply the fibre.

10 Continue to apply the fibre in this way under each loop of twine, teasing each handful of fibre so as to merge them as though applied as one application. Do this until you have covered the seat with fibre, and as you do so form both the depth and shape of the seat desired. The highest point of the seat/fibre should be just forward of the centre to provide the sitter with the feeling that they are sliding towards the back and not the front of the seat.

TIP: The outer edges of the seat should be of a higher density of fibre than the middle to help you form the firm edge at a later stage and to give a visible aspect of both the size and shape of the seat while at the same time supplying comfort to the centre.

Scrim/hessian

11 The fibre now requires a cover of either hessian or lightweight scrim, used here, which will both hold and form the shape of the seat. It is important the scrim is placed correctly, with the warp and weft of the scrim running parallel with the frame. The scrim should be applied using 13 mm (½ in) temporary fine tacks placed approximately 5 cm (2 in) apart and tacked the full length of the rail, up to the corners. Failure to do so may result in difficulty in forming the edge of the seat. Note that the scrim has been applied with a small tuck to provide strength and prevent thre threads fraying or being stretched.

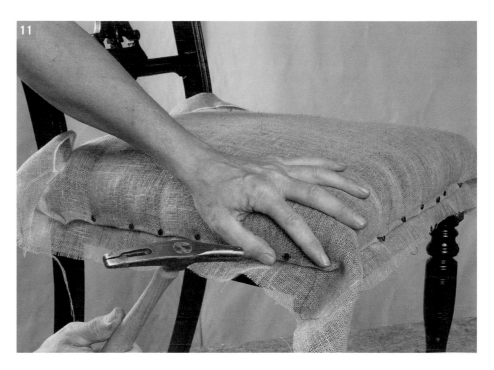

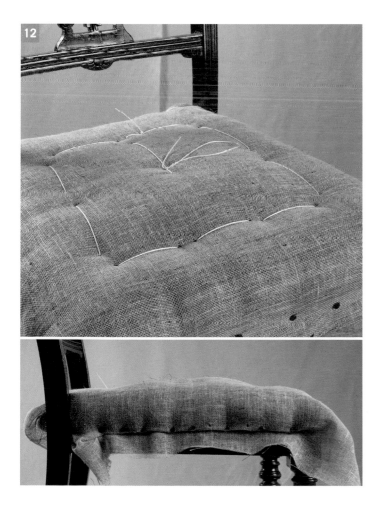

Stuffing ties

12 Stuffing ties are used as the final securing method to hold and control the stuffing in the centre of a seat, back or arm. They are applied over the scrim or hessian that covers the first stuffing. The ties, which can be applied using either nylon or natural twine, are inserted with a bayonet needle. Work your way around the seat, about 8 cm (3 in) in from the edge. Pass the needle down through all various layers and across approximately 2 cm (¾ in) on the underside before returning upwards. Form a slip knot with the two ends. Take the needle book down, 8 cm (3 in) distance from the first stitch, just as you would with a running stitch. Again leave a space of 2 cm (¾ in) on the underside and continue to sandwich the various materials until you have gone all the way round the seat. It is a good idea to bring one final stitch into the centre of the seat to ensure an even coverage, at which point you would tension the twine evenly and tie off. The layout of the ties is crucial: correctly positioned, they will ensure an even and equal tension over the whole area.

Re-stuffing and tacking down

13 The process of re-stuffing all four sides of the seat will form the basis for stitching the sides to form a very firm edge. This is done by removing the front rail temporary tacks and scooping more teased fibre underneath the scrim.

14 When enough fibre to make the edge very firm has been applied, use your hands to roll the scrim between the fibre and the frame to form the height and shape of the edge.

15 When tacking the scrim down permanently using 10 mm (⅜ in) fine tacks, you should ensure that you have achieved a secure fixing. Failure to do so may result in the scrim tearing away from the tack.

5–10 mm

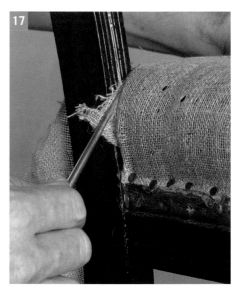

TIP: Placing the scrim perfectly square to the frame means you can take advantage of any edge that is parallel to the weave by following a line of thread in the scrim to help you tack down correctly. This will assist you in forming a neat and straight edge as well as producing the same height across the length of the edge.

16 The height and shape of the edge are achieved by rolling the scrim and pinching it between your fingers and thumbs. Note the slight overhang of the stuffed edge. If the edge is tacked down perfectly vertical, when the top fabric is applied an optical illusion will make it seem like it is falling back in towards the centre of the seat. In all these types of construction, it is therefore necessary that on completion the finished edge should slightly protrude forward/upward of the rail.

17 Note how the regulator is used to tuck in the edge of the scrim which can then be regulated to the required shape.

Stitching

18 For the edge of the seat to keep its shape two types of stitches are required to hold the shape and keep the edge firm. These are blind and top stitches, both of which start with a slip knot (see page 71). Start with a row of blind stitches slightly above the tacks.

19 Follow with a row of top stitches above the blind stitches (see page 72). This particular seat requires a single line of blind stitches and a single line of top stitches.

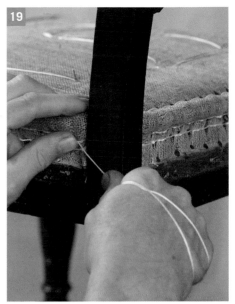

Bridal ties and second stuffing

20 To complete the shape and general finish, a second layer of bridal ties and mixed animal hair is required on the top surface of the seat. The hair is applied in the same way as the first stuffing (see Steps 9 and 10), but with smaller bridal ties and a much thinner layer of hair. The hair will remove any unevenness that earlier stitching may have caused.

Skin wadding

21 A layer of skin wadding is then placed over the top of the second stuffing to help prevent any hairs from poking through. This layer is only ever laid in place and does not need fixing.

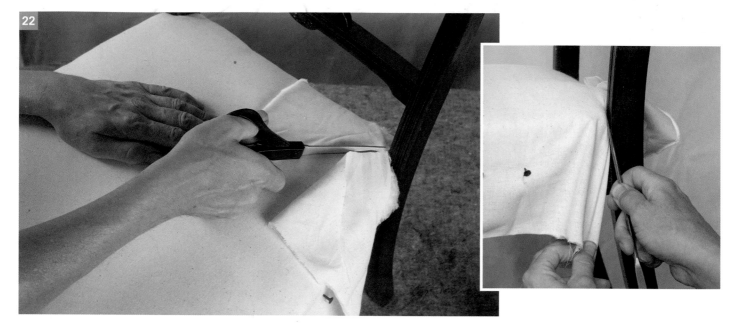

Calico

22 Now cover the whole of the seat with a layer of calico. As with the scrim, the calico is positioned so that it is parallel/square with the frame and is fixed using 13 mm (½ in) temporary tacks. Diagonal cuts are made to mould the calico around the two back legs and a regulator is used to tuck it neatly around the legs (see pages 62–64).

23 Releasing the front rail first, the calico is lifted and the hollow on the side of the stitched edge formed by the stitching is filled with either hair, linter felt or skin wadding (or two or more of the above), to form a very slight convex curve on the front of the seat. The calico is then permanently tacked down on the front rail with 10 mm (⅜ in) fine tacks to give the optical illusion that the face edge of the seat is flat and not concave. Repeat this process and tack down at the back then the side rails.

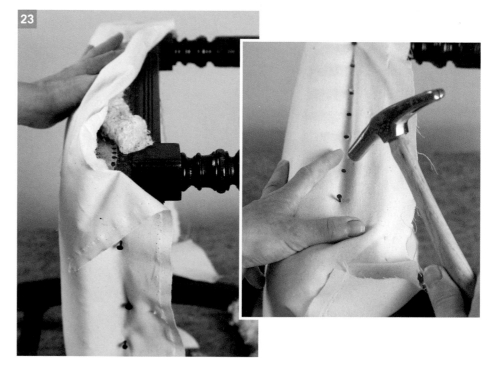

Top fabric

24 To complete the seat, a second layer of skin wadding is applied (but not fixed) under the top fabric to ensure that no fibres penetrate through to the surface. The top fabric is fixed using 13 mm (½ in) temporary tacks to set the fabric in position. It is then permanently tacked with 10 mm (⅜ in) fine tacks starting at the front, then back and sides, leaving the corners till last.

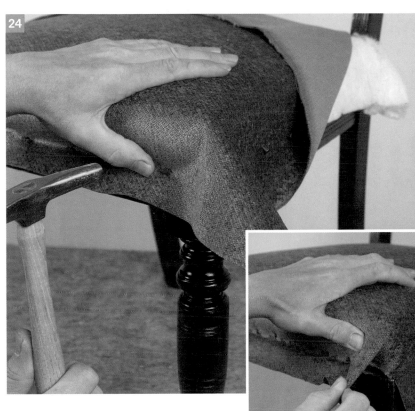

25 To ensure a straight, clean line, use a craft knife to trim the excess fabric. The fabric should be trimmed to just above the top of the show wood.

Bottom cloth and trim

26 Cut a rectangular piece of black lining and temporary tack it on to the underside of the chair. Trim to size, then turn a small amount of lining under and tack it approximately 5 mm (¼ in) from the edge of the frame using 10 mm (⅜ in) fine tacks. Place the tacks approximately 40 mm (1½ in) apart to complete the chair. Trim the lower edge of the upholstered frame using a decorative braid attached either with a hot melt glue gun or a suitable trimming adhesive. Apply the glue to the braid and press it down so that the bottom of the braid sits tightly against the show wood.

project 2

VICTORIAN NURSING CHAIR

The sprung chair was first developed in the mid-19th century, with the availability and standardisation of the double cone spring that we know today. This project introduces you to the art of hand springing and stuffing. As with many traditional pieces of furniture, sprung nursing chairs are still available in many forms today, using modern materials and spring systems.

Tools

- Upholstery hammer
- Upholstery scissors
- Wooden mallet
- Ripping chisel
- Web strainer
- Upholstery shears
- Tack lifter
- Pincers
- Trimming knife
- Rasp

Needle kit

- Regulator
- Double-ended bayonet needle
- Spring needles
- Semi-circular slipping needles
- Upholstery skewers
- Upholstery pins
- Tape measure and metre rule
- Tailor's chalk

Sundries and fillings

- Webbing
- Hessians
- Scrim
- Fibre
- Hair
- Calico
- Skin wadding
- Top fabric
- Bottoming cloth
- Various grades and sizes of tacks
- 4-cord or nylon twine
- Double cone springs
- Laid cord
- Glue for braid

Ripping down and frame preparation

If you are using an old frame you will need to remove the bottom cloth, then each layer of material. See pages 42–44 for further instructions.

Webbing

1 The webbing should be applied on the underside of the frame using 5 x 4 number of webs (see pages 45–49). Subject to the standard and condition of the frame either 16 or 13 mm (⅝ or ½ in) improved tacks should be used, with 16 mm being the preferred choice.

The position and spacing of the webs are important: the woven webs should be spaced and laid out running front to back in a slight fan effect and set parallel with the front rail of the frame in order to distribute the weight evenly and allow the accurate positioning of the springs.

Positioning the springs

2 Take a moment to choose the height and gauge of the springs for the project you are undertaking. In this particular project I have used five 12.5 cm (4 in) x 11 swg double-cone springs. This gauge is the mid point between seat and back springs and provides support as well as comfort in this type of chair. If you are unable to acquire this gauge, then 10 cm (4 in) x 10 swg is a suitable substitute.

The springs are placed in a central position to give maximum support and comfort. The number of springs and layout required is entirely dictated by the size and shape of the frame. The metal 'knots' at the top of the springs have been placed in an inside position to prevent wear on the spring hessian (the hessian that covers the springs). Had the knots been placed on the outer edge of the spring layout there is a good chance that the hessian would wear prematurely.

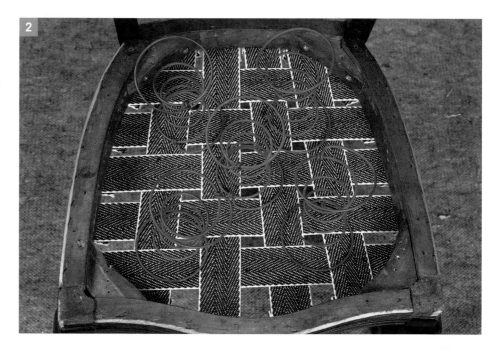

TIP: Always consider the position of the knots when applying these types of spring as it could affect the lashing of the springs (see page 58).

TIP: Choosing the wrong springs can result in your chair being too high or too low, too firm or too soft. If the chair is for yourself you can choose what you feel is comfortable to you, but if you undertake this as a commission talk and listen to your customer's requirements.

Securing the springs

3 Using a spring or curved needle, tie in each spring with four knots, starting with a slip knot, and ensure that each and every knot is pulled very tight. Secure the last knot on the spring with three knots (see techniques, page 71).

TIP: With the chair upright and grasping the top of the spring you should not be able to rotate the bottom ring, which is fixed to the webbing. If you can, then the ties have not been pulled tight enough.

Lashing the springs

4 The purpose of spring lashing using laid cord is to ensure the correct operation and movement of the spring so that throughout its life the spring will operate correctly and will be prevented from buckling or, worse-case scenario, snapping. This layout requires the springs to be lashed in a diagonal formation so ensure that all springs are lashed at right angles on each and every spring (see page 58). Other methods require back to front and side to side lashing to achieve the cross lashing formation. You can now see how the position of the knots on the top of the springs could have affected both the positioning and the tying of the laid cord.

Spring hessian

5 With the springs now secured in position and able to act as a unit, we can now apply a layer of 340-g (12-oz) or heavier hessian. This will form a platform over the springs to allow the application of the first stuffing. Start by cutting a piece of hessian approximately 8 cm (3¼ in) larger than the frame, allowing for the curvature of the springs.

6 Now place the hessian over the springs and temporary tack it at the front, back and sides, removing all fullness and allowing it to cover the springs.

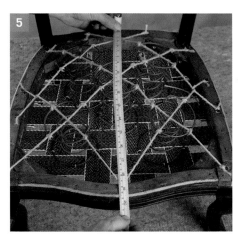

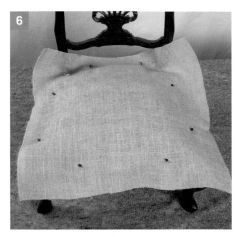

7 This will position the hessian and allow you to permanently tack it down with 10 mm (⅜ in) improved tacks. Note that the corners are folded and pleated diagonally around the posts, so that no cutting is required for the corners.

TIP: When applying any type of fabric, such as hessian or top fabric to any shaped parts of furniture, you will only be able to follow what are called 'corridors'. This means that any visible threads and/or patterns will flow through the centre back to the front or from side to side, resulting in the threads/patterns outside these corridors flowing evenly away to the corners. (See pages 65–67).

Securing the hessian

8 To prevent excess wear on the hessian caused by the friction of the springs rubbing against the hessian, sew the hessian to the springs. This is done using the same method and stitch used to sew springs to webbing, using a spring or curved needle and 4-cord/nylon twine.

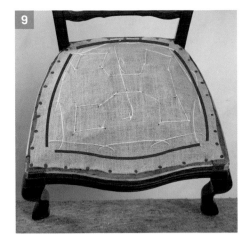

Bridal ties

9 You now have to apply the bridal ties. This is done in a similar way to Project 1 (see Step 8, page 82) but this time taking into account the dome created by the springs and the shape of the frame. Note how the outer ties follow the shape of the frame and how all the ties are laid out to give maximum coverage and to ensure that the springs are covered.

First stuffing

10 When applying stuffing over springs, you should ensure there is sufficient fibre not to feel the springs through the stuffing. Overstuffing will result in the seat looking like the top of a balloon rather than a gentle dome shape. The highest point of the seat should be just forward of the centre and the outer edges should be of a higher density of fibre than the middle.

TIP: As a general guideline, to work out if you have the required amount of fibre over the springs, place your hand with your fingers outstretched on the top of the seat and press down. If you can only just feel the springs, you know you have the correct amount of fibre required to cover the springs. The fibre will compact when the scrim is applied forming a good protective and comfortable layer over the springs.

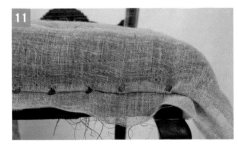

Scrim/hessian

11 Now cover the seat with either lightweight scrim or hessian, using 13 mm (½ in) temporary tacks, which will both hold and form the shape of the seat. As with the spring hessian it is important to apply the scrim/hessian using the corridor method (see page 67). Failure to follow this procedure will result in a poorly constructed edge.

Stuffing ties

12 The ties are applied in a similar method to Project 1 (see pages 78–87) but care should be taken to ensure that only the two layers of scrim/hessian are sandwiched and that the springs and lashings are not interfered with in any way. Note the layout and positioning of the ties which follow the outline of the frame and are positioned approximately 7.5 cm (3 in) in from the edge. This provides maximum control and coverage to the seat.

Re-stuffing and tacking down

13 Ensure you have positioned the scrim parallel to the frame. This will allow you to use the weave of the scrim to form the correct height and shape that is required when tacking down. This picture shows the shape of the frame as you would see it from the underside of the chair – note the shape.

14 Here you see the thread line that needs to be achieved after the scrim has been tacked down – look closely at a single thread along the front edge and you will see that it follows the outline of the frame in and that at any two mirrored points on the front rail the thread is in an identical position.

Look at the side rail from the underside of the frame: it curves downwards at one end so when tacked down, the threads of the scrim should follow the same curve as the underside of the frame.

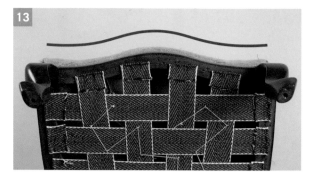

TIP: When constructing stitched shaped rails a slight enhancing of the curves can give a superior look to a chair. A stitched edge is usually finished with a slight protrusion. The way to achieve this on this or similar shaped rails is by very slightly overhanging the convex part of the edge and very slightly bringing the concave section to an almost upright position. This will give a very distinct line on the finished seat.

Stitching

15 Blind and top stitches should now be applied (see page 72). Unlike Project 1, you cannot follow the thread of the scrim here to achieve a straight line. Professional craftspeople call upon their years of experience, but for those new to upholstery I recommend that you use tailor's chalk and draw evenly spaced lines on the side of the scrim, using the frame as a reference. This will help you form lines of stitching parallel with the frame, which will lead to straight stitching and an evenly stitched edge.

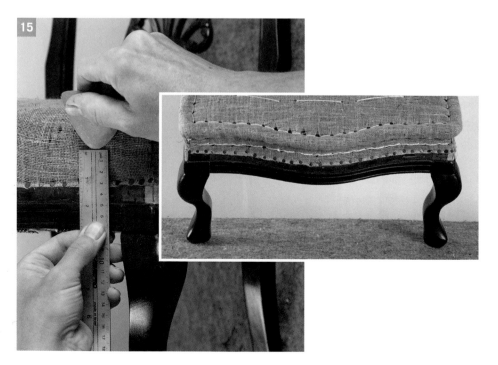

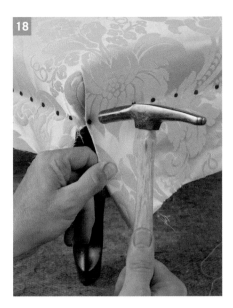

Bridal ties and second stuffing

16 To complete the final shape and finish of the seat, apply a second set of bridal ties and mixed animal hair, then a layer of skin wadding over the top, as described in Project 1 (see Steps 20 and 21, page 85).

Calico

17 As with Project 1, the calico is applied using the same principles, but taking into account that you have no straight edges to follow you must apply the calico using the corridor method (see page 67). The threads of the calico will act in the same way as the scrim and will naturally follow the contours of the seat. Permanently tack the calico into position.

Top fabric

18 To complete the seat a second layer of skin wadding is applied under the top fabric to ensure that no fibres can penetrate through to the surface. The fabric is tacked using 13 mm (½ in) temporary tacks to set the fabric in position. It is then permanently tacked using 10 mm (⅜ in) fine tacks. Make a single corner pleat on the two front corners.

Bottom cloth and trim

19 Cut a rectangular piece of black lining and temporary tack it on to the underside of the chair. Trim to size, then turn a small amount of lining under and tack it approximately 5 mm (¼ in) from the edge of the frame using 10 mm (⅜ in) fine tacks. Place the tacks approximately 40 mm (1½ in) apart to complete the chair. Trim the lower edge of the upholstered frame using a decorative braid attached either with a hot melt glue gun or a suitable trimming adhesive. Apply the glue to the braid and press it down so that the bottom of the braid sits tightly against the show wood.

MODERN DEEP-BUTTONED STOOL

The application of buttons or tuffs to form a decorative finish or to enhance the shape of part of a chair has been around since before Victorian times, although it was the Victorians who popularised what we know today as deep buttoning. Buttons and/or tuffs can be applied in two ways. The first, and easiest, method is known as 'stab' or 'star' buttoning. This is where a button is inserted and pulled down through the fabric and compresses the stuffing to a depth where the top of the button is just below the surface of the line of fabric. This may form a ripple effect in the fabric around the button but is not meant to form any pleating. The second method, covered here, is deep buttoning. This is where the fillings and fabrics are purposely constructed to allow the fabric to form both the pleats and diamond pattern.

Tools

- Upholstery hammer
- Upholstery scissors
- Wooden mallet
- Ripping chisel
- Upholstery shears
- Tack lifter
- Pincers
- Trimming knife
- Rasp
- Staple remover
- Staple gun
- Foam drill
- Foam saw
- Buttoning machine

Needle kit

- Regulator
- Double-ended buttoning needle
- Semi-circular slipping needles
- Upholstery skewers
- Upholstery pins
- Tape measure and metre rule
- Tailor's chalk

■ This project will introduce you to the art of deep diamond buttoning and will describe the construction of a simple suspension system, the cutting and preparation of the fillings, and how to mark out, cut and apply fabric.

Sundries and fillings

- Hessian
- Foam
- Reconstituted foam
- Polyester wadding
- Top fabric
- Calico
- Bottoming cloth
- Various grades and sizes of tacks and staples
- Foam glue
- Nylon twine
- Serpentine springs, clips and nails
- Laid cord
- Buttons
- Decorative nails

Preparation

1 As with all upholstery frames, whether new or old, ensure the frame is in good condition and any sharp edges and splinters are removed so that no damage can be done to yourself or the materials you are using. It is also advisable to protect any show wood, in this case the legs. An old pair of socks slipped on and secured with masking tape is a great way of protecting them.

2 Because the re-upholstery materials used here are modern, serpentine or zigzag springs make an ideal choice. Start by marking the point at which the retaining clip for each end of the spring will be fixed. The clips should be placed at a maximum of 10 cm (4 in) centres along the longest rails of the stool. The last clip should be placed approximately 15 cm (6 in) in from the outer edge of the side rail. Fix each clip with a barbed nail to position it flush with the inner edge.

3 The springs can now be measured and cut to size. To do this measure between the clips and allow a very small allowance for the upward curve of the springs.

4 It is important that you kink the ends of the springs to prevent restriction of movement and the clips slipping out before applying the springs.

5 Place one end of the spring into the clip furthest from you and hammer the clip closed. This is done for safety reasons as you will be stretching the spring towards yourself to engage it into the opposite clip. Use a length of webbing folded in half lengthways to aid with stretching the spring. There is a chance that if the spring is not properly secured, it may disengage from the clip and fly towards you, resulting in potential injury. As you apply each spring, hammer the clip closed at both ends. When all springs have been applied nail down each clip to permanently secure each spring in place. If working on a small frame, the back of the frame may lift under tension when applying the springs.

6 This type of spring is designed to move in an up-and-down motion only, so it is vital that the springs are restricted from moving from side to side. To ensure this, lash the springs from side to side using laid cord.

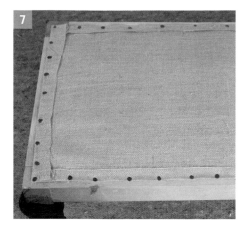

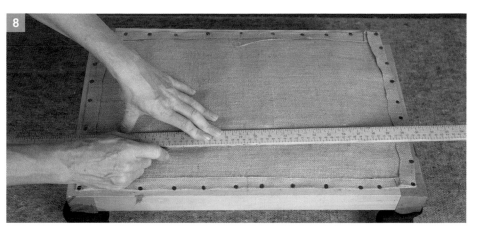

7 The springs require a covering of hessian, 340 g (12 oz) being the minimum weight you should use. Apply 10 mm (⅜ in) improved tacks or staple the hessian in place to cover both the springs and clips but leaving the outer top edge of the rail exposed.

8 Before proceeding the background of the button layout should be drawn onto the hessian. The size of the diamonds is determined by the size, shape and style of the piece that is being upholstered. The diamonds can be large or small but in the main, they are always higher than they are wide. For instance 15 x 10 cm (6 x 4 in), 18 x 12.5 cm (7 x 5 in), 20 x 15 cm (8 x 6 in). Great care should be taken when positioning the anchor points of the buttons. On this occasion I have chosen large diamonds measuring 20 x 14 cm (8 x 5½ in). Using tailor's chalk, start by drawing two central lines on the hessian: one vertical and one horizontal. All other lines will be measured from these two lines. Measure 10 cm (4 in) on either side of the central horizontal line and draw two parallel lines.

9 Measure 14 cm (5½ in) on either side of the central vertical line and mark the top and bottom horizontal lines with a small dash, as shown here.

10 Using a ruler, draw diagonal lines between the dashes to form the diagonal lines of the diamonds.

11 The background must now be transferred to the reverse side of the hessian. To do this poke through the cross point with a needle or regulator and mark with either tailor's chalk or a wax crayon.

TIP: Do not use marker pens to transfer the marks as the ink can sometimes transfer onto other materials, such as the top fabric.

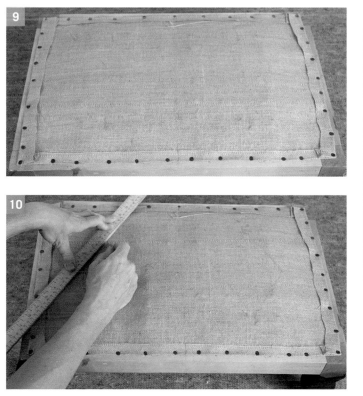

Constructing and applying the filling

12 The filling now needs to be prepared. Here 5 cm (2 in) thick RX39 foam has been firmed up at the sides by gluing a 2.5 cm (1 in) border of reconstituted foam (commonly know as chip foam) to the outer edges. This is commonly known as walling. To do this, measure the size of the frame and reduce the measurement by 5 cm (2 in) in both directions: this is the size of the RX39 you need to cut. Now cut strips of chip foam 5 x 2.5 cm (2 x 1 in) and accurately glue these to the sides of the RX39. This will bring the size of the foam back up to the original measurement and will provide a firm edge to the filling.

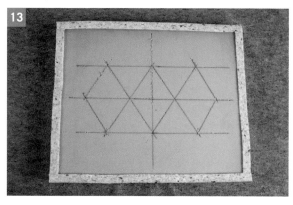

TIP: When applying foam to a frame or board, always ensure that it is accurately cut to the correct shape. It is always better to have a very slightly oversized rather than undersized filling, which can be trimmed if necessary.

13 On what will be the underside of the foam, mark out the same buttoning background as on the hessian. These marks will provide the position of where you will drill or bore out the foam, to allow the buttons to pass through it and be anchored to the hessian.

14 The foam now needs to be accurately drilled so that the holes are at the exact point where each button is to be placed.

TIP: When applying almost any type of foam to a spring system, a layer of thin felt or some other thin, dense material should be placed between the foam and the springs to prevent wear and prolong the life of the materials.

15 Once all the holes have been drilled attach the foam to the frame. There are several ways of doing this. You can glue calico flies to the foam, then tack or staple them to the frame; staple the foam directly to the frame; or, as in this case, glue the foam directly to the frame.

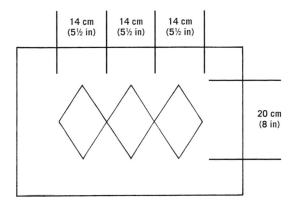

14 cm (5½ in) 14 cm (5½ in) 14 cm (5½ in)

20 cm (8 in)

Background measurements

Note the difference between the two sets of measurements: one set for the background and another for the fabric, incorporating any allowances. Note that the fabric measurements relate to the buttoned area only and do not take into account the fabric required from the outer buttons outwards.

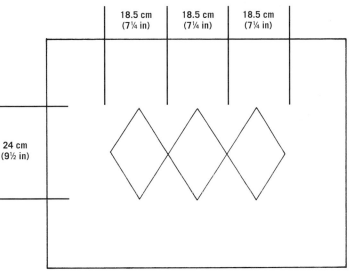

18.5 cm (7¼ in) 18.5 cm (7¼ in) 18.5 cm (7¼ in)

24 cm (9½ in)

Fabric measurements

NOTE: These allowances are, in the main, universal but variations will be required when working with different types of material, such as leather or a knitted fabric. When working on concave shapes (which require reduced allowance) or convex shapes (which require increased allowance), these calculations can only be achieved through trial, error and experience.

Preparing and cutting the cover

The cover now needs to be prepared and cut. Draw a rectangle on an A4 sheet of paper to represent the outline of the fabric. Draw the button formation of the stool inside this rectangle and add all the dimensions you require to mark out the fabric. Take the measurements of the diamonds on the cutting sheet, which will include the allowance that is required to form the pleats and the amount of fabric needed to tack off on the underside of the frame. Be aware that the average amount of allowance required for each diamond is an additional 4 cm (1½ in) in the height and 4.5 cm (1¾ in) in the width. This allowance is based on an average depth of 5 cm (2 in) of filling. This may not appear to be logical as to the shape and size of the diamonds but it is necessary to prevent or reduce the tears that may form across the diamonds. The depth of the filling and the thickness of the frame can vary greatly, therefore the measurements from the outer ring of buttons must be measured with a tape measure and cannot be set by the allowances used. All markings should only be made on the back of the fabric.

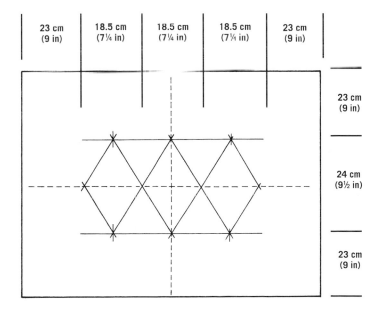

23 cm (9 in) 18.5 cm (7¼ in) 18.5 cm (7¼ in) 18.5 cm (7¼ in) 23 cm (9 in)

23 cm (9 in)

24 cm (9½ in)

23 cm (9 in)

Applying the top fabric

16 The top fabric is now ready to be applied. Prior to doing so a layer of polyester wadding with button holes punched through it must be placed over the foam. Cut 45 cm (18 in) lengths of nylon or six-cord buttoning twine and a 7.5 cm (3 in) length of webbing for each button that is to be applied. Place a button on a length of twine and pass both ends through the eye of the buttoning needle. Starting on the line of buttons along the long side of the stool, do the following:

a) Push the needle through the top fabric where a button is to be placed. Pass the needle through the hole in the foam, then through the same positioning point on the hessian.

b) Pull the needle all the way out and leave the twines hanging out the underside of the stool.

c) Position the fabric and while pulling on both twines, push the button and fabric down into the hole. Form a slip knot with both ends of the twine, roll up the webbing along the long side and place the webbing between the twines. Finally, slide the slip knot up until the button is tight against the hessian which is being anchored by the webbing.

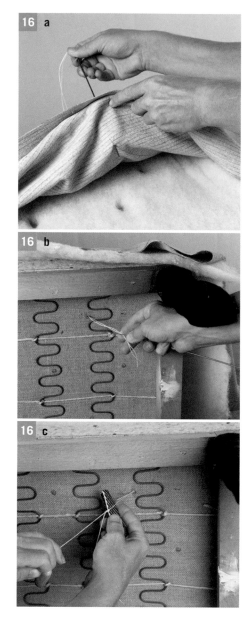

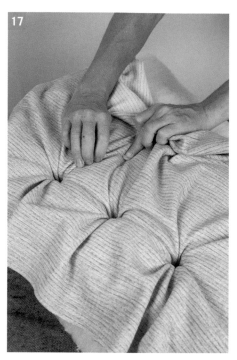

17 Repeat until you have secured a line of buttons. Before continuing to the next line, use both your fingers and a regulator to roughly form the pleats. It is important that the pleats are positioned and lying in the correct direction. All diamond pleats will lie in one direction but subject to the top fabric used, could be laid from the centre outwards to form a uniform look. The next row of buttons can now be applied. Continue to follow this procedure until all the buttons have been inserted.

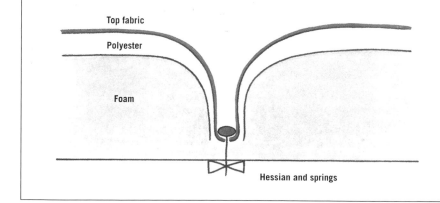

Top fabric

Polyester

Foam

Hessian and springs

This diagram demonstrates how the button is pulled down through the hole in the foam and anchored with a web tuft.

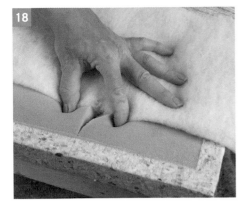

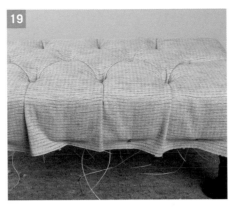

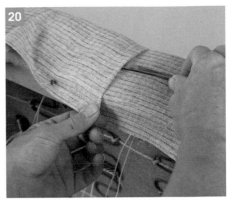

18 After completing the application of the buttons, fold the fabric on all sides in towards the centre of the seat to expose the surrounding edge of the foam. Using a long-bladed knife, cut a 45-degree slit out towards the edge into the foam and then into the polyester on each outer button. Make the slit in the direction of the pleat you will later make from the button to the underside of the frame. Repeat this operation with each outer button, ensuring the cut is in the correct position to form the pleat.

19 The fabric can now be re-laid over the foam. Ensure the fabric is positioned correctly between each button. Failure to do so will result in some or all pleats having either too little or too much fullness within them. As you position the fabric and form the pleats, place a temporary tack on the underside of the frame between each pair of pleats.

20 Using a regulator, manipulate all the pleats in to their final position, then, starting from one end, permanently tack the pleat nearest a corner, tension the fabric both across and away from the next button and place a permanent tack to form the pleat. Usually you would continue with this method until you have reached the centre of the frame and then start from the opposite end and work back towards the centre, which would mean that if you had a central pleat it would be the last to be fixed. With smaller items of furniture that do not have many pleats, as with this stool, this rule may not apply.

21 To finish, cut the fabric to allow it to form around the leg. Finish with either double or single corner pleats (see pages 69–70).

22 Finally, apply a black or dark coloured lining to the underside of the seat to provide a neat finish. Decorative nails can be used to finish off the corners of the seat if you so wish.

MORE ADVANCED BUTTON LAYOUTS

The stool is the simplest form and style of deep buttoning and the one upholstered on pages 96–103 has been centrally positioned with an even number of buttons, but there can be many variations to the button layout. When deciding on the configuration and shape of the layout, consideration should be given to both the style and shape of the part of the chair that is being buttoned. The following should be taken into account:

• Does the height of the back require the button layout to be central? In many cases the measurement from the top button to the top edge of the frame is often shorter than the measurement from the lowest button to the bottom of the back. This provides a pleasing aesthetic look to the finish, whilst also taking into account the space that a cushion will take up.

• Does the shape of the back require the same number of buttons on each row? If, for example, you are working on a shaped back, such as a balloon back chair, then you would aim for the distance from each outer button to the edge of the frame to be approximately the same.

• Does the width of the diamond remain constant on all horizontal lines? A tub chair back normally fans out slightly as it increases in height, and therefore the inner circumference would increase. This would require the width between the diamonds on the lowest line of three to be slightly narrower (about 5 mm (¼ in)) than those on the top line.

Examples of some of these layouts are found below.

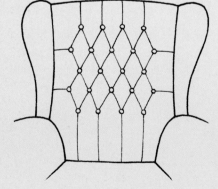  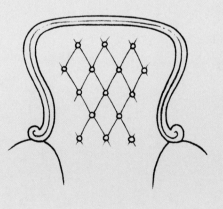

Various types of button layouts

Van-dyking

Van-dyking is the method of joining fabric widths for diamond buttoning. The joins will be hidden behind the pleats that form the diamonds. The most basic method of van-dyking is shown here. The fabric is marked out on the reverse side and on reaching one side of the fabric, two sets of lines have been draw. The inner solid line on both pieces of fabric are the machine lines, while the outer dotted lines are the machine allowance and where you would cut the fabric to shape and size.

When machine stitching the two or more pieces of fabric together it is imperative the button points match. Failure to do so may result in badly shaped or lined diamonds and/or misalignment of patterns. This method of van-dyking works for any straight run and so there is no limit as to how many pieces can be joined together.

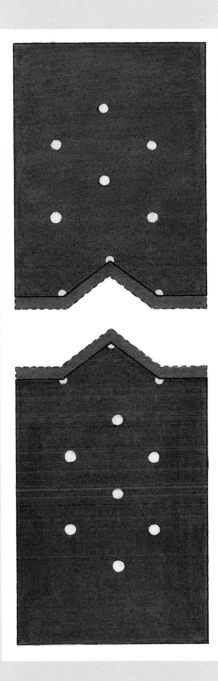

project 4
MODERN HEADBOARD

There are many methods of producing modern upholstered headboards, which involve the use of a variety of materials, including wood, metal and plastics. The earliest types of headboard were probably a form of hanging tapestry. In more modern times, towards the beginning of the 20th century, headboards were constructed of polished wood, some very simple, others more elaborate. As with many design ideas, they tend to go full circle and resurface using new materials, but the traditional style of headboard is still in popular demand.

Tools

- Upholstery hammer
- Upholstery scissors
- Wooden mallet
- Ripping chisel
- Upholstery shears
- Tack lifter
- Pincers
- Trimming knife
- Staple remover
- Staple gun
- Foam saw

Needle kit

- Regulator
- Upholstery skewers
- Upholstery pins
- Tape measure and metre rule
- Tailor's chalk

Sundries and fillings

- Foam
- Polyester wadding
- Top fabric
- Bottoming cloth
- Various grades and sizes of tacks and staples
- Foam glue
- Back tacking card

■ This project will guide you through the construction of a headboard using board material as a base and modern materials, such as foam and polyester for the filling. The design here is of a basic shape but involves most, if not all, the techniques required for this type of construction. More elaborate designs may require a variation on some of the methods used.

Preparation

1 In my professional opinion the best board material to use is plywood that is a minimum of 12 mm (½ in) thick. A slightly thicker board may be required if working on a double bed sized headboard. One of the advantages of plywood is its strength and versatility. The board can be of a low quality with an unfinished surface, as none of it will be visible on completion. This headboard has a slightly oval shape, with a bordered edge and decorative cord finish. Start by accurately marking out and cutting the board to the required shape and size, and sand off any sharp edges, splinters or any other debris that could damage the fabric or affect the final finish. Measuring from the outer edge of the board, draw a line 12.5 cm (5 in) in around the sides and top of the board: this is the width of the border you will apply later.

Applying a guide strip

2 Staple a 12 mm (½ in) wide strip of mounting card, plywood or hardboard 2 mm (¹⁄₁₂ in) thick on the inner edge of the line you have drawn. This will serve as a guide for the staples or tacks to ensure a clean, straight line between the centre panel and the border. This is called the 'guiding edge'.

3 The inner panel is now ready for the foam application. The foam should be cut to size so that it includes the width of the strips. To cut the foam to the correct size, first cut a paper template to the exact size and shape of the foam required. Place the template on a sheet of 4 cm (1½ in) thick RX33 foam and cut out the shape with either a foam cutter or, alternatively, an electric carving knife. Do take the appropriate safety measures when using either of these tools.

4 Bevel the edges of the foam. This can be done using one of two methods. The first is to bevel the edges using a pair of upholstery scissors; the second is to use a foam cutter or an electric carving knife. Place the foam on a cutting table. Place a strip of plywood over the foam and rest the blade against the edge of the table and the edge of the plywood to achieve a regular bevelled edge.

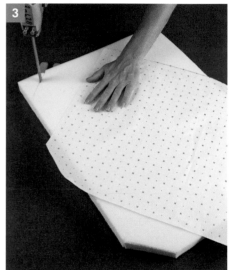

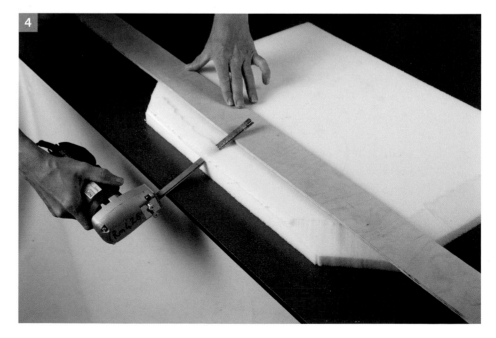

5 Glue the foam to the board with the bevelled edge on the underside, ensuring that you cover the narrow guide strip applied earlier. Make sure, however, that the edge of the strip is still visible to avoid an uneven line between the inner panel and the border.

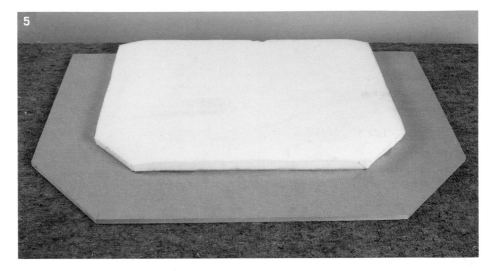

6 The foam is now covered with a layer of either 70 or 115 g (2½ or 4 oz) polyester wadding. The wadding should be slightly larger than the foam. The edges of the foam should not be exposed and the wadding can be trimmed if necessary.

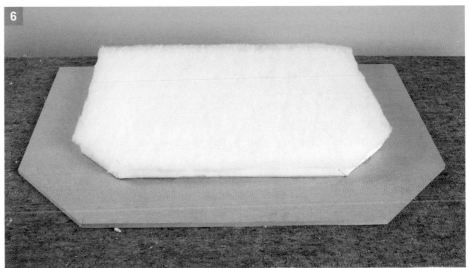

7 Cut the first piece of fabric slightly larger than the size of the foam panel you are covering. I would recommend a 5 cm (2 in) allowance on each side. Lay the fabric over the foam and temporary tack in to position around all edges, ensuring any pattern or graining is straight and correctly positioned. Be careful where you place the tacks as you don't want holes in the fabric.

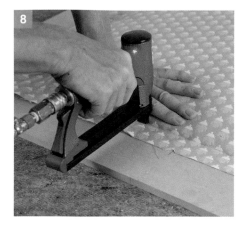

8 Once you are satisfied that the fabric is correctly positioned, ease and manipulate it in to a clean line and permanently fix it using the staple gun by rubbing the nose of the gun against the guiding edge to form a straight edge. Alternatively you could use tacks: feel for the guiding edge and hammer the tacks in a neat line. Finish the bottom of the fabric by permanently tacking it to the back of the board. Trim all excess material from the edges.

9 We now move on to the border. You will need to fix the fabric to the board before applying padding to the border. To do this, cut strips of fabric wide enough to take into account the depth of the stuffing and tacking allowance needed for all sides. In this case you will require five pieces of fabric. Starting at the top, place the middle section fabric of the border on the board, wrong side up, on top of the stapled centre panel with the ends folded in. The amount of fabric that you fold in should take into account the outward angle of the pleat that you form later, allowing a 12 mm (½ in) tacking surface. Staple the fabric into position. Repeat this operation with each section of fabric but only folding the end that is not overlapping the previous panel. Allow excess fabric at both ends to take into account the outward angle required when fixing the opposite side of the fabric.

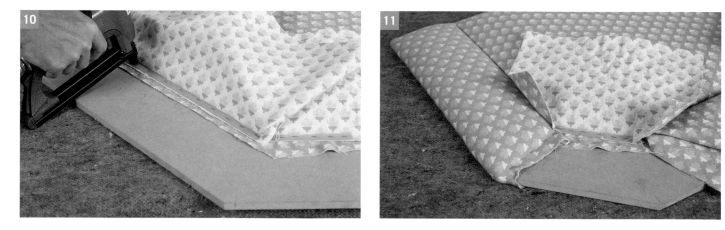

10 Now place a piece of back tacking card, or, if unavailable, a 12 mm (½ in) strip of mounting card over the fabric of each panel. This will form the clean, straight edge between the centre of the back and the border. Push the card tightly against the guiding edge and staple it into position.

11 Cut five pieces of 2.5 cm (1 in) thick RX39 foam to shape and size, allowing the width of the foam to roll over all the outer edges of the plywood to form a soft rounded edge. Bevel the underside of the inner edge of the foam in the same way as the centre panel foam. Carefully glue the foam pieces into position, one at a time, on each section of the border, taking care not to get any glue onto the fabric. Cover the foam with a layer of polyester wadding. Starting with the lowest panel, pull the cover over the foam and permanently fix the fabric to the back of the board. Apply a row of staples to the inner corner and trim any excess fabric before applying the next piece of foam.

12 On attaching the next panel up, form the pleat into the correct position over the first panel. Continue to fix the fabric in this way, alternating each side.

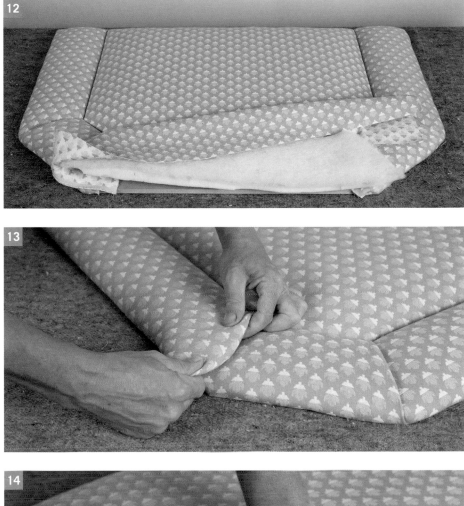

13 The final middle panel will require pleats to be formed at both ends. Neatly fold the fabric under the foam to form a pleat, then staple the fabric to the back of the board.

TIP: The tension of the fabric is normally sufficient to hold the pleats in place, but if this is not the case, then the pleats can be slip stitched.

14 The decorative cord can now be fixed into place. Start by stapling/tacking the cord on the reverse of the headboard. Lay the headboard flat and using a hot melt glue gun (taking care in respect of health and safety), place a line of glue approximatcly 7–10 cm (3–4 in) long in the grove between the border and the centre panel. Pull the cord across the glue and press it in to position. Repeat this operation until you reach the other end of the groove and finish by stapling/tacking the end of the cord on the back of the headboard.

The rear of the headboard can be finished with a lining to provide a neat finish. The choice of colour is not vital, but a dark colour is recommended. The lining can be stapled/tacked on but for a more professional finish it should be hand sewn on.

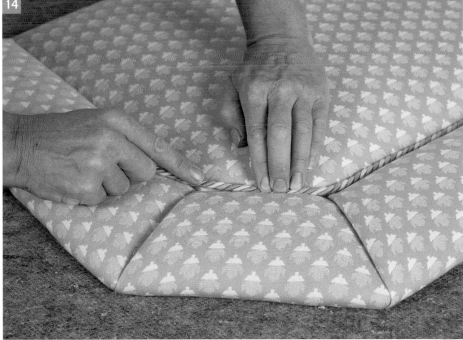

project 5

CHILD'S CHAIR

This project is an ideal practical exercise, which will follow on from the earlier seat constructions (Projects 1 to 3). It will introduce to you the importance of understanding the connections between different parts of a chair, in this case the back and seat, whether traditional or modern. You will use a combination of traditional stuffings, some of which have been modernised, as well as modern suspensions and fillings. The design and standard of the frame used here allows for adaptation inasmuch as additional shaped pieces of wood can be added to the frame to enhance its shape, along with the possibility of attaching arms.

Tools

- Upholstery hammer
- Upholstery scissors
- Wooden mallet
- Ripping chisel
- Upholstery shears
- Tack lifter
- Pincers
- Trimming knife
- Rasp
- Staple remover
- Staple gun
- Foam saw

Needle kit

- Regulator
- Semi-circular slipping needles
- Upholstery skewers
- Upholstery pins
- Tape measure and metre rule
- Tailor's chalk

Sundries and fillings

- Webbing
- Hessian
- Foam
- Reconstituted foam
- Polyester wadding
- Top fabric
- Calico
- Bottoming cloth
- Various grades and sizes of tacks and staples
- Foam glue
- Nylon twine
- Serpentine clips, springs and nails
- Laid cord
- Back tacking card
- Decorative nails

Frame preparation

1 Because this is a new frame, the rails may have sharp edges which should be smoothed down with glass paper. This will prevent damage to the various materials you will be applying, especially the top fabric. Make sure all show wood is protected before commencing. Here, the legs have been protected with two pairs of old socks.

Construction of the inside back and back webbing

2 With any style of chair, the back requires good support to ensure the filling that is attached to it will maintain its shape and resilience and provide the comfort it has been designed for. To have an understanding of how much force is placed on a back, consider any individual person's weight and imagine that it has to support something in the region of 40 per cent of that weight. Use 5 cm (2 in) wide webbing: rubber or elasticated webbing are both fine. The webs should be placed no further than one and a half web's distance apart, or 7.5 cm (3 in) (see pages 45–49). Elasticated webbing has been used here and the webs have been stapled in place Because of the slight curvature of the back, the horizontal webs are not woven but placed underneath the vertical webs.

Back hessian

3 The webbing now needs to be covered with 285 g (10 oz) hessian. Cut the hessian slightly larger and tack it to the inside back of the frame using 1 cm (⅜ in) improved tacks. Note how pleats have been placed in each direction of the hessian to allow the movement that elasticated webbing provides.

Rubberised hair

4 Had jute webbing and hessian been applied under tension, then bridal ties, hair and scrim would now be applied but because this is a modern piece, rubberised hair has been used instead. Measure the area you wish to cover and cut the rubberised hair 5 cm (2 in) larger than required. Place in to position, skin-side-up, and staple the very edge of the hair to the bottom rail of the back, leaving 5 mm (¼ in) of the rail exposed. This will later be filled with the next layer of filling and allow you to form a clean edge. If required, a very small amount of loose fibre can be tied in behind the rubberised hair to enhance the shape. Ease the hair up and over the top rail and staple 5 mm (¼ in) in from the back edge. Now ease the rubberised hair round the side rails, again 5 mm (¼ in) in from the back edge and staple in place.

5 Using a sharp craft knife, carefully hold down the excess rubberised hair and trim off the excess material, cutting very close to the staples.

Linter felt and wadding

6 A layer of linter felt needs to be applied over the rubberised hair, followed by either skin wadding or polyester. When applying felt and similar materials, only cut or break off the excess filling, as it is better to remove the majority of the excess now and trim more accurately later, when permanently fixing the fabric to the frame.

TIP: An alternative to linter felt is foam – a very acceptable alternative in this type of construction. In this particular case I would recommend RX30 foam which will provide softness as well as support.

Applying the back fabric

7 Using a tape measure, calculate the amount of fabric required by taking the vertical measurement first, followed by the horizontal measurement. Ensure that you have sufficient fabric to both grip and pull with as well as being able to tack the fabric in the required position. As you can see in the drawing, the fabric has been cut sufficiently long enough so that it will eventually be tacked onto the top of the seat rail, directly in contact with the seat fabric. It is very important to take where the fabric is fixed into account when two or more parts of the same upholstered piece of furniture come together (i.e. back and seat). You need to be fully aware how these parts join together and how they will interact with each other when in use. Failure to do so could result, for instance, in a gap forming between the back and seat.

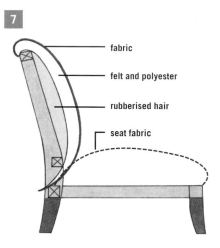

fabric

felt and polyester

rubberised hair

seat fabric

8 Start by laying the cover over the back and temporary tack on the inside face of the seat rail. Pull the cover upwards and temporary tack on the rear of the top rail, ensuring any pattern, stripe or graining is positioned correctly. Finally, temporary tack the sides of the fabric to the rear of the upright rails, taking care not to tack where visible damage to the fabric will be seen on completion. The fabric may need some final adjustments, but should now be under the correct tension and position in preparation for any cuts that are required and for final fixing. With practice this can often be achieved quite easily, but may require several attempts and adjustments for those with limited experience.

9 Using blunt-ended scissors, cut the fabric on the inside of the upright post. This will allow the fabric to pass between the upright post and be re-temporary tacked on top of the seat rail. Make sure that the cuts are the correct length: the end of the cut should sit tightly where the upright post and the underside of the lower back rail meet. Temporary tack in place.

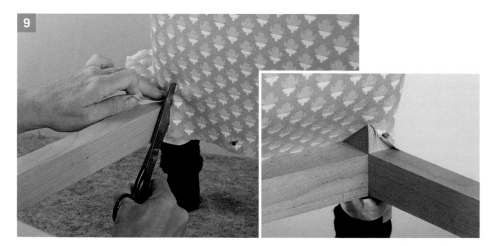

10 Once the fabric has been re-attached to the top of the seat rail, proceed to the top rail and release the tacks along the top only. Lift the fabric and trim the felt and polyester to fit snugly in the groove left by the rubberised hair, up to the top edge of the rail. Re-pull the fabric and permanently fix it to the rear of the rail, ensuring you have a smooth and level finish to the top of the chair and a clean outer edge. The top corners should be completed only when the top and sides have been permanently fixed. Proceed to one side of the chair back and repeat the process as with the top rail. You will find that extra tension will be required by pulling the fabric downwards and backwards diagonally on the lower half of the side. This will help form the shape of the lower back and remove any excess fullness that has accumulated due to the changing shape that is being formed. This action and method is known as the pulling point.

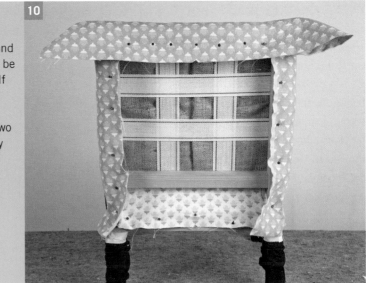

TIP: The line across the back where the seat and back meet must be taut and clean. If this is not the case, the finish between these two components may be very poor.

11 To finish the back, complete the corners by applying double corner pleats (see page 70). The lower back now needs to be released and temporary tacked up on the rear of the lower back rail.

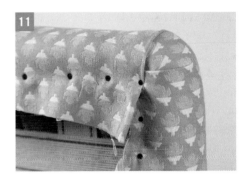

Constructing the seat

12 The seat is constructed using rubber or elastic webbing and will be applied as described on pages 48–49. This chair requires four webs back to front and three webs side to side.

Seat hessian

13 The webbing now requires a covering of 285 g (10 oz) hessian. As with the back, cut the hessian slightly larger and tack it to the top surface of the seat rails using 1 cm (⅜ in) staples or 1 cm (⅜ in) improved tacks. A pleat needs to be placed in the hessian to allow for movement.

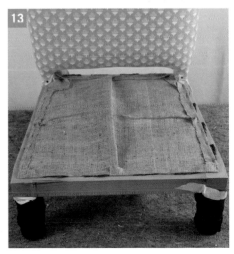

Foam cutting and lamination

14 The foam for the seat should be constructed using the following types of foam: a base of 5 cm (2 in) thick 5 lb reconstituted foam topped with 1.25 cm (½ in) thick RX39 foam. To cut and laminate the foam to the required shape, you can use one of two processes. You can place a marked out and cut-to-shape paper template on an oversize piece of foam and cut to that shape.

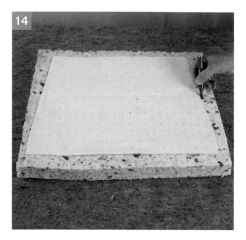

TIP: Either method of cutting and laminating works well, but if a number of chairs are to be produced I would recommend that the template be reproduced using a board material, such as fibre or hardboard. Be accurate with the cutting and application of both the size and shape of the foam, as this will aid you later and provide a superior finish to the chair.

15 Alternatively, you could laminate the different layers of foam together, which should again be cut slightly over size, then applied to the seat and marked out to the correct shape and size. Remove and trim.

The method you choose will be dictated by the type of frame, upholstery or suspension system already applied. For instance, a seat that is domed will require the foam to be cut larger to take into account the curvature.

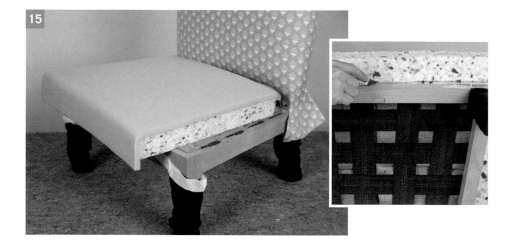

16 After cutting the foam to the required shape, cut a piece of 1.25 cm (½ in) thick RX39 foam 15 cm (6 in) smaller than the seat, to match the shape of the seat and glue it to the underside of the seat foam. The foam is positioned slightly forward of centre to maintain the forward position of the highest point of the seat. When the seat is applied, it will form a dome in the centre. This is usually only required if the foam is applied to webbing or other flat supports. Fix the foam to the frame with either a spray or spreadable adhesive.

17 The foam should then be covered with 115 g (4 oz) polyester wadding. Use a single layer of wadding on the top of the seat and a double layer on the sides to provide a smooth finish without bulking out the upright edges.

Applying the seat fabric

18 Finish the seat by capping on the fabric. Cut a rectangular piece of fabric 5 cm (2 in) wider than the maximum width required to allow for trimming in preparation for machining. The fabric should be sufficiently long enough to be tacked under the front seat rail and to pass through under the back to reach the back seat rail. Make sure you allow for extra fabric for gripping and pulling the fabric when tacking down. Jam the fabric down the back of the seat and temporary tack it to the underside of the front rail. If you have cut and applied the foam accurately this task is less arduous.

19 On the reverse side of the fabric, carefully mark the edge of the seat with tailor's chalk and identify the point where the fabric folds around the front edge of the seat.

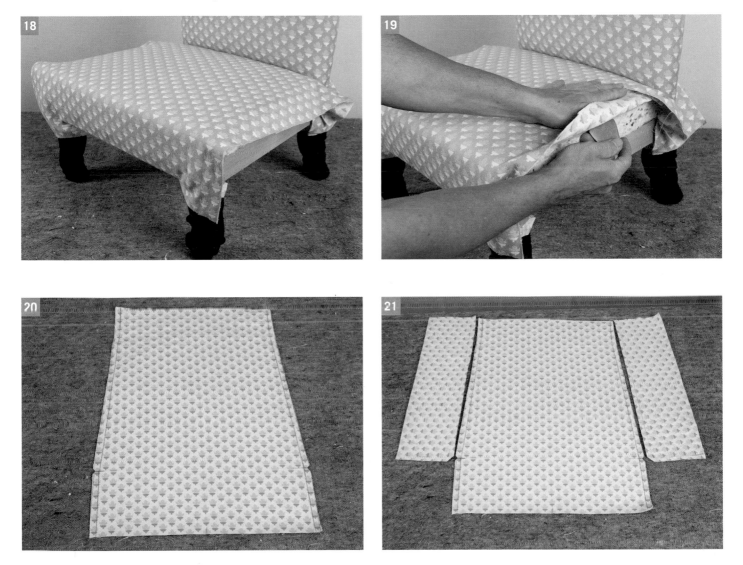

20 Remove the fabric from the seat and lay it out wrong-side-up on the cutting table. Using a ruler, measure out 1.25 cm (½ in) along the edge of the fabric and draw a line parallel to the chalk line applied in Step 19: this is the machine allowance. After trimming this piece of fabric to shape, ensure that the notch out is cut to identify the point where the fabric folds down the front of the chair.

21 Now cut two rectangular pieces of fabric, taking into account any pattern or pile, which will form the side borders of the seat. Make sure you add an allowance for tacking and matching.

22 You will also require two lengths of fabric to form the piping. These need to be 4 cm (1½ in) wide and slightly longer than the top seat panel. In larger items of upholstery, a join may be necessary but it is advisable to avoid this if at all possible. The fabric should be cut on the bias at about 45 degrees. Depending on the type of fabric you may feel that it would be better to cut either across or up the fabric to achieve a better finish.

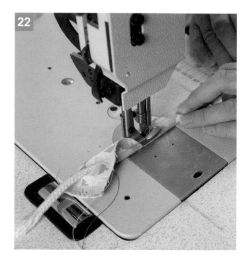

23 Apply the piping to the seat fabric, then notch out the piping so that you can clearly identify the corner point.

24 Place the border with the right side up on the machine bed. Lay the seat cover on top of the border, making sure that the notch is lined up with the corner of the border. Machine stitch together and repeat with the other border.

25 Check that the machined fabric is level and the corners are in the correct and parallel position. Place the fabric onto the seat and fix into position by temporary tacking to the underside of the front and side rails and by pushing a small amount of the fabric down the back of the seat. Before making any cuts in the fabric to allow it to pass either side of the vertical back post, it is important that the fabric is correctly positioned in its final position.

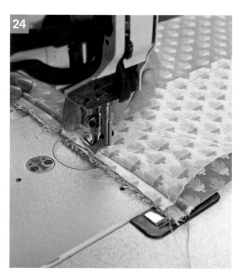

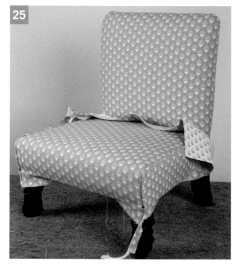

26 Make two Y cuts in the fabric (see techniques, pages 62–64): the first long cut on the inside of the post and the second, a small diagonal cut to allow the border to wrap around the post. These cuts will allow the fabric to pass between the back and seat and enable you to temporary tack the fabric to the back seat rail.

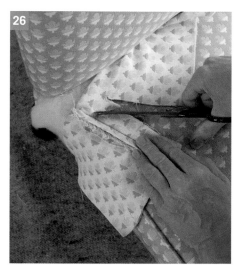

TIP: Be constantly aware of where the polished parts of the frame are, as you do not want to accidentally place tacks in this area.

27 Take care to cut the fabric to the correct length, and position allowing the fabric to sit snugly around the rail and preventing the possibility of either the cuts showing. If the fabric is under cut it will not pull into the correct position or back far enough. In this particular case you are not only fixing the fabric but are ensuring you have achieved the correct tension and fixed the fabric into its original position from when you first marked it (see Step 18). To finish fixing the fabric, re-pull and fix the fabric along the front rail, cutting around the front legs.

(see Step 18)

TIP: It is advisable not to complete the fixing of the fabric around the legs until the sides have been set and fixed.

28 The sides of the seat now need to be tacked down. You will need to find the pulling point at the rear of the border and using a fair amount of force, stretch the fabric back and slightly downwards. This will result in the weave of the fabric being slightly distorted, but in doing so will give a very clean finish to the side, cutting around the front and back legs as required. Permanently fix the fabric to the underside of the frame. The front corners should now be trimmed, folded in and fixed down. The tacks, gimp pins or staples can later be finished with decorative nails or braid.

29 To complete the seat, re-pull the seat at the back if necessary and fix to the rear seat rail. Check that the seat fabric is acceptable, with clean, distinctive lines. When satisfied release the bottom of the back fabric that was previously temporary tacked and permanently fix it onto the top of the seat to close any gaps between the seat and back. Any small gaps can be filled with polyester, which should be placed between the back fabric and bottom back rail. Again, pay particular attention of the line between the seat and the back.

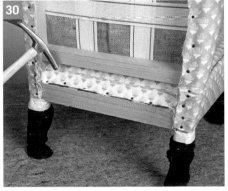

30 Trim and turn both fabrics to form a fold and re-tack together. This will form a secure fixing for both layers.

Applying outside back lining

31 The outside back of the chair needs to be lined with 285 g (10 oz) hessian. Start by turning the hessian inwards with a small fold and staple or tack along the lower edge of the top back rail, folding the ends in both directions in preparation for the fixing of the sides. Now pull the hessian downwards, starting in the middle and working outwards in both directions and fix it along the central point of the bottom rail. No fold is needed here because it may leave a ridge showing through the cover. Fold in one of the sides of the hessian and fix it to the inner edge of the rail. Repeat this on the opposite side, stretching the hessian in order to achieve a taut surface.

Applying outside back fabric

32 Cut a rectangular piece of fabric 5 cm (2 in) larger than the finished size of the outside back, ensuring that any pattern match and/or pile is accounted for. Lay the fabric wrong-side-up and position the material so that 1.25 cm (½ in) is positioned and fixed with staples or tacks.

33 Place a piece of back-tacking card so the upper edge of the card is fractionally below the top edge of the rail and fix it into place starting in the middle and work out towards the ends.

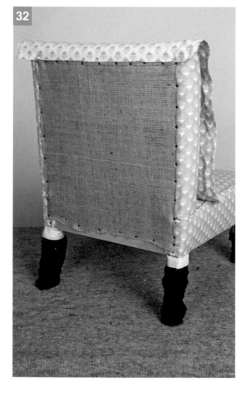

34 As you approach the ends of the card, trim them to the length required and nip any sharp edges from the card. Note how the ends of the card are slightly cut at an angle to help form the side folds.

35 Using a few fixing points, place a piece of polyester or skin wadding over the hessian, making sure that the card is well covered and that it can't be felt through the fabric. Trim the sides so they are set back 1.5 cm (⅝ in) from the outer edge of the frame. This will prevent problems when hand sewing the fabric. Finally allow the polyester to wrap around the edge of the frame, but cut any excess away around the legs to safeguard the fabric. Fold the sides of the fabric inwards and fix prior to pulling the cover over and down.

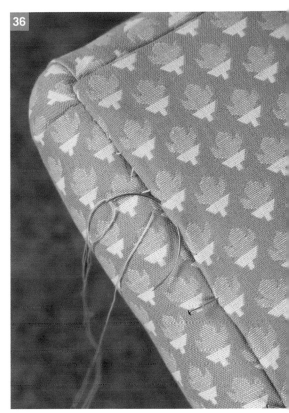

36 Temporary tack the fabric on the underside of the seat rail and pin the sides into position, slightly back from the edge. Cut around the legs and fold and fix the fabric into position. To complete the sides, slip stitch the fabric (see page 73). Re-pull and permanently tack the bottom of the back.

Bottom cloth

Apply as per Project 1 (see Step 26, page 87).

project 6

BOXED OR BORDER CUSHION

Amongst the skills an upholsterer needs to undertake a wide range of projects is the ability to use a sewing machine. Knowing its capabilities, interchangeable parts and how to use it safely are all very important. This project requires the use of a sewing machine and you should be fully acquainted with its workings. The boxed, or border cushion as it is known, will introduce you to the application of various panels of different shapes and sizes, fitting a zip and applying a decorative finish, in this case, piping. This project can be taken to a more advanced level by using fabric that requires pattern matching.

Tools

- Sewing machine (preferably industrial)
- Metre rule
- Scissors
- Un-pick
- Piping stick
- Continuous zip or medium- to heavy-duty nylon zip

Needle kit

- Tailor's chalk or pencils
- Pins

Sundries and fillings

- Machine thread
- Piping cord
- Foam cushion
- Polyester
- Top fabric

Marking and cutting the fabric

It is always advisable to unroll the fabric and check for any faults that naturally occur in the weave of the fabric. To do this you will need a large cutting area. In most small workshops upholsterers will have a cutting table usually 1.5 m (5 ft) wide x 1.2 to 1.5 m (3 ft 9 to 5 ft) deep. This should allow you to cut most of the panels you will need. When cutting patterned or large quantities of fabric a longer table is always better to assist you in seeing the larger picture.

Unroll the fabric on the table and square off the cut end of the roll. This can be done in three ways.

1a The first is to place the salvage edge on one side against the edge of the cutting table, place a tee square against the table side and draw a line across the bottom of the fabric with tailor's chalk.

1b The second method requires you to line up the material with the edge of the table and hang the fabric over the edge. Using the flat edge of the chalk, draw along the edge of the table to provide you with straight squared fabric, which can then be trimmed.

1c The third method is to pull away lines of the weft thread until a full width thread is removed, after which the warp threads can be trimmed.

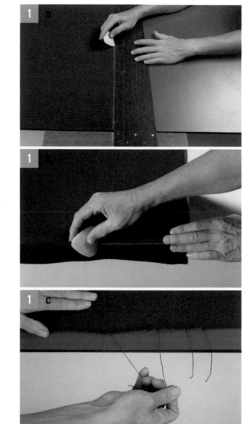

2 The cushion being made here is rectangular. Start by marking out the top and bottom panels. The fabric has a 1.5 cm (⅝ in) sewing allowance on all sides and the piping has a width of 4 cm (1½ in). Note that the marking out is done on the right side of the fabric to allow you to check the fabric for flaws, and where necessary, patterns. Take care when measuring, as not all chalks and similar fabric-marking equipment can be easily brushed away. Next, mark out two sets of borders and a zip border, of which the width will be made up of two halves. These will be cut slightly wider, to allow trimming to the correct width after the zip has been made up. Also mark out the front and side borders and finally the material required for making up the piping, which should be cut on the bias. Double check that all panels are correctly marked out before cutting.

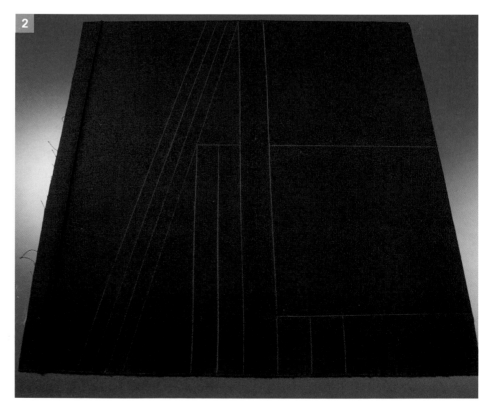

TIP: There are some professional differences in how a cushion is constructed and the cutting/application of the piping. The chart below explains some of these differences:

	Upholstery	Soft furnishing
Cutting piping	Usually cut on the bias but the fabric may dictate that it needs to be cut across or up the roll.	Always cut on the bias to allow maximum flexibility.
Applying piping	Usually applied to the top and bottom panels first.	Usually applied to the pre-machined borders first.
Borders/joints	Depending on the style of the chair (i.e. chair with or without arms), borders will wrap around corners and will be joined on the sides.	Borders are always joined on corners.
Zip	Depending on the chair, upholsterers tend to bring the zip a short distance around each side to allow easy insertion of cushion.	Zip borders are normally joined on the corners.

Sewing the cushion panels together

3 To begin, machine all the lengths of piping together to form a single length that is long enough for each side.

4 The piping is now made up in preparation for attaching to the top and bottom panels. Because the piping fabric was cut to a specific width and machined correctly, you will automatically end up with a 1.5 cm (⅝ in) sewing allowance. Position the piping flush with the side of the top panel, leaving a short length of piping beyond the foot of the machine which will be sewn later when you join the two ends of piping together.

5 Make sure that when the piping is attached to the front of the cushion no join will be along the front edge. Machine the piping along the edge of the fabric until you almost reach the corner. Snip the machine allowance on the piping with sharp-tipped scissors.

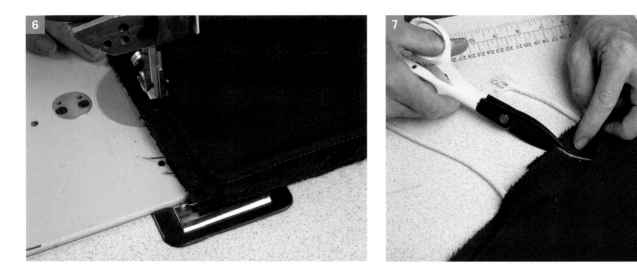

6 Continue to machine the piping until you reach a point of approximately 2 cm (¾ in) from the corner. Ensure that the needle of the machine remains down through the fabric, lift up the foot and rotate the top panel 45 degrees towards you. Pull the piping round so that it is positioned diagonally across the corner, lower the foot and apply two or three stitches. I recommend that you achieve this by manually turning the machine hand fly wheel. Lift the foot again, leaving the needle down and repeat the process of turning the fabric and piping. This will bring the fabric into position to machine the front edge. Repeat the corner process until you meet up with the other end of the piping.

7 Where the two ends of the piping meet, overlap one with the other and cut the excess off, leaving approximately 7.5 cm (3 in) over length. Undo the machining of both ends of the piping to facilitate trimming the fabric to the correct length, open the fabric flat and lay the end that you started with, which will have a diagonal cut, under the opposite end of the piping. Trim the top layer to match the diagonal cut of the other piece but with a 3 cm (1¼ in) overlap. This will give you the machine allowance for joining the piping together.

8 Join the piping in the same way as above. Flatten out the join and cut the piping cord to length so that it butts together tightly. Finish attaching the piping to the top panel. Repeat this process to apply the piping to the bottom panel.

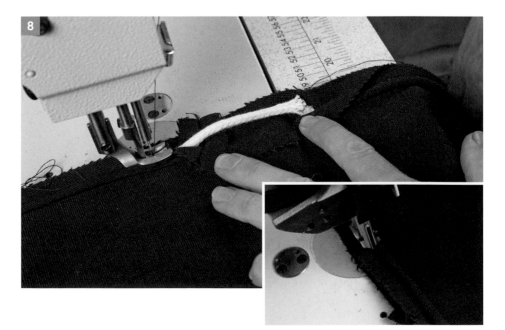

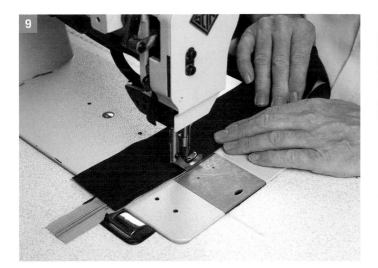

9 Before applying the borders, the zip border needs to be assembled. Professional upholsterers use what is known as 'continuous zip'. This usually comes in 100 m (328 ft) rolls and is cut to the required lengths, and the slider is added after the zip border is made up. If this is not available, then a pre-made medium- to heavy-duty nylon zip is perfectly acceptable. Start by checking the border is sufficiently long enough to cover the length of the back edge of the top panel and is able to return around the corners by a minimum of 10 cm (4 in) on each side. This will allow for the machine allowance required and a small amount of excess that can be cut off later. The zip should be cut a further 10 cm (4 in) longer to allow insertion of the runner. To attach the zip to the border, machine the cover with the wrong side up parallel with the edge of the fabric.

10 Fold the border over so as to cover half the teeth of the zip and re-machine the border.

11 Now repeat this operation to achieve the other half of the zip.

12 The slider should now be applied. This can be achieved by cutting away some of the teeth at the end of the zip, as shown here.

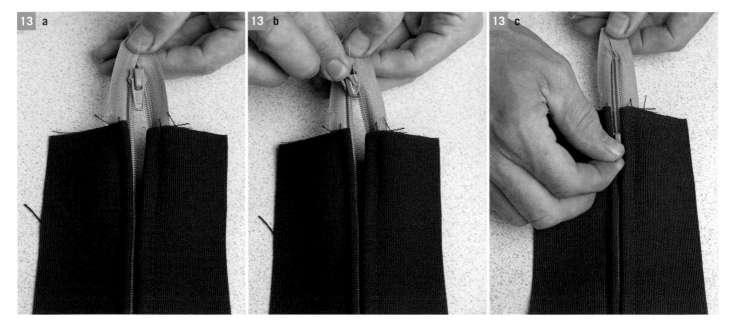

13 The runner has an equal amount of zip inserted in the slots on either side.

Holding the crossed-over tape firmly, grip the slider.

Now draw the slider in towards the centre of the zip border. It is now ready to be applied to the cushion.

14 Using tailor's chalk and a ruler, measure, mark and trim the border to the correct width in preparation to attaching the top panel.

15 The cushion is now ready to be assembled. On both the top and bottom panel, mark or notch out a point 7.5 cm (3 in) in from the back corner on the side of each panel. This is the point where the zip border will join the plain border.

16 Now lay the full width front border on to the top panel and centralise it so that equal amounts of fabric are down each side of the top panel. Mark or notch out this position. It is normal that you will require short extensions of the front borders in order to marry up to the zip borders. Note that in all cases a machine allowance plus some additional excess material must be added to the length of all borders.

TIP: When assembling a cushion in this way it is easier to cut all the borders longer than required. They can always be cut to the required length at a later stage. Trim and join the borders as you apply them to the top panels.

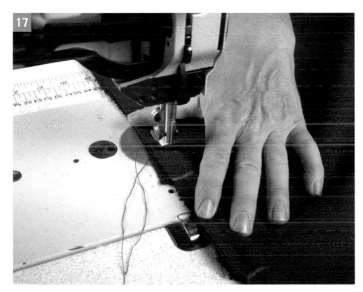

17 To apply the borders, start with the top panel, wrong-side-up, laid on top of the end of the front border at the joining point previously marked, allowing for sewing allowance that you will need when you come to join the other end of the border. Using the sewing line that attached the piping as your guide and ensuring all panels are parallel at the edge, machine the border to the top panel. On reaching the corner, make several small cuts in to the border to allow you to form the corner of the border, as done previously with the piping.

18 Continue to apply the front border until you have negotiated all corners and have reached the next notch where the next section of border is to be added. Remove the fabric from the machine and lay the border that has been sewn to the top panel flat, trim to length if required, again allowing for the machine allowance. Machine the small extension that is required to make up the length of the front border and continue to apply to the top panel until you reach the next notch.

19 At this point, attach the zip border. To do this, follow the same procedure as Step 18 but with one addition: the join between the plain side border and zip border needs to be top stitched. This will provide a reinforced join, which will prevent the slider from being pulled off the end of the zip when opening or closing, and will flatten the join to achieve a professional finish. Continue to follow this process until the border is complete, forming the completed top and side borders.

20 Prior to applying the bottom panel, a series of notches must be applied to ensure that both the top and bottom panels are aligned. To align the panels, fold the border fabric at each corner, as shown here, ensuring that the border is parallel, and **NOT** as shown in the inset picture.

21 Note that these notches, when positioned for machining, identify the machine corners of the border (main pic) and not the outer edge of the fabric (inset pic). If neither of these correct procedures is followed, the panels will not line up and the result will be a poorly made cushion.

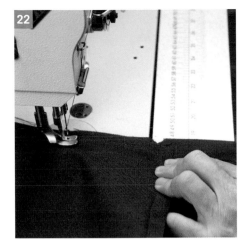

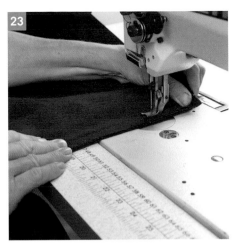

TIP: The notch method described in this construction can be used in multiple ways to identify various points when machining, where two or more pieces of fabric need to marry up and fabric corners are few or non existent (i.e. a cushion that has a square front and round back).

For instance, as can be seen in the diagram below, small notches have been placed on the curved side of the cushion, (these notches are applied in identical positions on both the top and bottom panels). These notches allow you to position the border to the bottom panel, ensuring that both top and bottom panels are aligned.

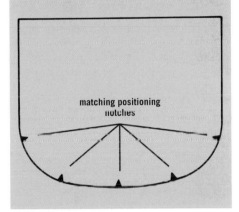

matching positioning notches

22 The bottom panel can now be sewn to the partially completed cushion. Start on one side of the cushion, near to the front corner, with the border underneath the bottom panel. Line up the notch with the corner and, starting approximately 10 cm (4 in) back from the corner, machine towards the notch. As you approach the corner apply small cuts to allow you to turn the corner as before.

23 After turning the corner, pin together the panel and border to line up the next corner and notch together. Pulling at this point should remove any small amount of excess tensioned fullness that may have accumulated in the machining process. Stretch all panels/piping equally.

24 With the fabric still secured by the machine needle and holding the pinned point under tension with your left hand, grasp the top panel/border with your right hand. Maintaining the tension at a comfortable position, release your left hand and machine the short section together. Repeat this process until you have reached the corner. Continue to use this technique until you have completed the application of the bottom panel. Note that where the borders are joined at each corner the joins replace the notches.

To turn the cushion the right side out, pull apart the zip on one side of the slider and place your hand inside the cushion. Open the zipped area fully and turn the cushion right side out.

DAY BED

The day bed is the forerunner of the modern-day chair or sofa that has an extended seat to allow the sitter to raise their legs while at the same time sit in an upright but comfortable position. This particular style of day bed is also sometimes known as a backless chaise longue. It is a popular misconception that the part that you lean on is referred to as the arm and in many ways, because it is often placed against a wall, this is an understandable mistake, but ideally it should be positioned in a bay window or conservatory and therefore the arm should be referred to as the back. This project describes the assembly of a traditionally constructed sprung scroll back, and the forming of an under-the-edge finish incorporating a plywood facing and a sprung seat, which will expand your experience of hand springing.

Tools

- Upholstery hammer
- Upholstery scissors
- Wooden mallet
- Ripping chisel
- Web strainer
- Upholstery shears
- Tack lifter
- Pincers
- Trimming knife
- Rasp

Needle kit

- Regulator
- Double-ended bayonet needle
- Spring needles
- Semi-circular slipping needles
- Upholstery skewers
- Upholstery pins
- Tape measure and metre rule
- Tailor's chalk

Sundries and fillings

- Webbing
- Hessians
- Scrim
- Fibre
- Hair
- Calico
- Skin wadding
- Top fabric
- Bottoming cloth
- Various grades and sizes of tacks
- 4-cord or nylon twine
- Double-cone springs
- Laid cord

Frame preparation

This project is made using a new frame. All sharp edges should be sanded down with glass paper and the outer edges around both back scrolls and the top outer edge of the seat should be planed or rasped to a 45-degree angle. You will require a pattern of the back facing: paper is acceptable but card is preferable. Label and store it for later use.

Constructing and webbing the back

1 Before applying the webbing, note the shape of the back; it has a curved, concave shape flowing into a scroll. Should the webs be applied vertically the shape of the back would be lost. It is therefore imperative that the horizontal webs be applied first and reinforced with two or three vertical webs, which should not be over strained. Note that the vertical webs are placed over the horizontal webs and not woven. This ensures the shape of the back is maintained while providing the required support. Note the positioning of the folded ends of the webs, which have been set towards the centre of the rail, leaving the outer edge clear for other materials.

Applying the hessian

2 The webs on the back now require a covering of 385 g (10 oz) hessian. Cut the hessian larger than required to allow for pulling tight; it can be trimmed to size later. Because of the slightly curved shape of the back frame, turn the back edge of the hessian to form a fold, and using 10 mm (⅜ in) improved tacks or staples, fix the hessian down onto the upright posts following their shape, while at the same time leaving the outer edge of the posts clear. Now stretch the hessian towards the front, tack down, trim, fold the hessian over and re-tack. Then ease the hessian both up and down and tack to the top and bottom rails, leaving the outer edge of the rails clear.

TIP: In this particular case, a higher tension should be applied to the hessian from the front to the back, and only eased from top to bottom. This will maintain the shape you are trying to achieve. This method of stretching fabric around a curve should be used whenever a concave or convex shape is to be achieved.

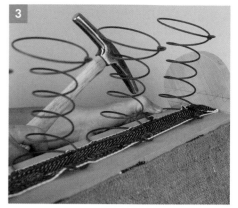

Applying the back springs

3 Fold the ends of a piece of webbing and place it full length on the top of the scroll spring rail and tack at each end. Position double-cone springs under the webbing. The springs should not be placed more than 5 cm (2 in) apart. Slide four 10 cm (4 in) x 12 swg double-cone springs underneath the webbing, with the knot of the lower ring positioned on the inside of the frame. This is done to allow maximum coverage by the fibre, which will prevent wear and the possibility of feeling the knot on the surface. The two springs at either end should be positioned so that they are approximately 4 cm (1½ in) or two fingers' width in from the inside of the upright posts. The remaining springs should then be evenly spaced between these two springs. To fix the springs use eight 13 mm (½ in) improved tacks, which should be tacked through the webbing at four equal distances apart: four on the inside of the spring and four directly opposite the first set on the outside of the spring. Be careful not to damage the webbing when applying the tacks and ensure that the springs are firmly secured to the frame and cannot move.

4 The tops of the springs now need to be stabilised but must also be allowed to move up and down in the correct manner. Tack a piece of webbing to the top of the scroll on one side of the back using 13 mm (½ in) improved tacks and ensure the web is lined up with the centre of the springs. Using your own strength only and not a web strainer, pull the webbing across the top of the springs and tack it to the top of the opposite scroll. This should form an even and gentle curve to the top of the back.

5 The springs may require slight repositioning. As you do so, tie the springs with four-cord and a curved or spring needle, starting with a slip knot on the four most outer corners of the webbing as it passes over each spring.

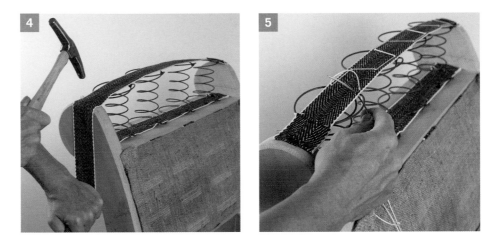

TIP: It may be necessary to sew the springs at either end at a slight angle, leaning either towards the front or rear of the post, depending which is nearest. This will enable the spring to return to an upright position when compressed. To check whether a spring is in the correct position, hold the spring and webbing together and compress the spring: the spring should, when compressed, be in an upright position. If it isn't, re-adjust the position of the spring until this is achieved.

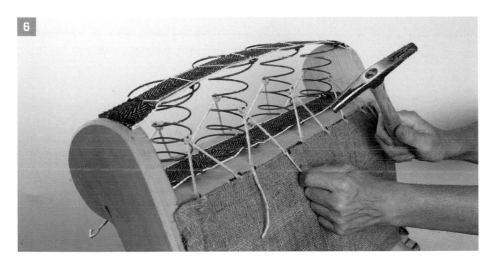

6 Now that the springs have now been stabilised from the front and back, you need to do the same to prevent any sideways movement. Cut a piece of laid cord long enough and form a clove hitch knot approximately half way up the height of the spring and form an inverted V that can be tacked using 13 mm (½ in) improved tacks into the side of the spring rail (the cord is wrapped around the tack which is then hammered in to secure the cord). This must be done on both sides of each spring. Note that you should only take up any slack in the laid cord, as the spring has already been put under tension by the top webbing. Failure to do so could result in the spring leaning towards one side. Trim the excess cord.

7 A second piece of webbing now needs to be placed on the outside of the scroll. This, unlike the top webbing, should by applied using a web strainer. The purpose of this web is to initially help form the outside of the back and to extend the longevity of both the shape and life of the construction.

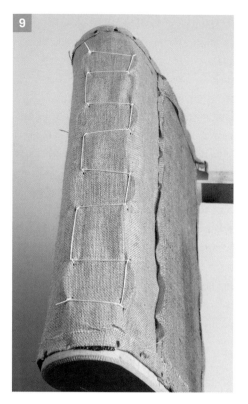

Applying spring hessian and ties

8 The springs should now be covered by 340 g (12 oz) or heavier-grade hessian, fixed with 10 mm (⅜ in) improved tacks. When positioning the hessian, the horizontal central corridor that passes from side to side runs across the top centre of the scroll over the webbing. On this occasion the vertical corridor runs over the middle of the back, allowing the threads of the hessian to fall downwards equally at both ends.

9 The hessian should now be fixed to the springs using four-cord at four equal points on each spring to reduce wear on the hessian.

10 Using four-cord, bridal ties should now be applied over the whole of the back. There is no set way as to whether they should be set vertically or horizontally, but in this case a line of ties has been sewn vertically parallel to the edge of each scroll, from the bottom rail to the underside of the spring rail. This will provide a base for applying a balanced amount of fibre to the edge, which will be stitched to form an edge later. The remaining ties are placed horizontally, with two ties positioned along each top edge of the springs to ensure that the edges of the spring wire are covered with fibre.

Applying fibre

11 Fibre should now be applied. Because this is a back and not an arm and has mirrored and equal size facings, the amount of fibre that should be applied on one side must mirror the other in size, shape and density. Additional filling will be required to form a higher density of fibre along the whole length of the top of the back, as this area will receive most punishment, although the back should not be sat on or leaned against but is often used in this way. The fibre should be applied so that when the scrim is temporary tacked into position, the shape and size of the back will look almost finished.

Appling the scrim

12 Using a fabric tape measure, calculate the amount of linen scrim required. Form a fold in the scrim and, following a thread line, line up the scrim with the edge of the rail and temporary tack it to the inner face side of the seat rail. Starting in the centre and working outwards, temporary tack the top of the scrim to the underside of the spring rail by pulling the scrim with one hand while easing it with the other. Remove the first line of tacks you applied on the lower rail and re-pull the bottom of the scrim to achieve the vertical (through the centre of the back) and horizontal (across the top of the back) corridors. Once you have achieved this, temporary tack down the sides of the scrim, gathering around the scroll as necessary. As described later in this project, you can start to see the cartwheel effect form on the facing (see inset). On this type of finish – a double-ended scroll – it is very important that the back should be the correct shape and size as it will be very difficult to make any major alterations at a later stage. Rub the flat of your hand firmly across the whole of the back and feel for any lumps or hollows within the fibre. In nearly all cases any bumps and hollows can be rectified with a regulator.

Applying the stuffing ties

13 The stuffing ties should now be applied to sandwich the fibre and two layers of hessian/scrim. It is important that these ties are placed correctly to ensure a good finish.

Tacking down the back scrim

14 The sides of the back, known as facings, will be constructed with an under-the-edge finish in preparation for a plywood facing which will be inserted at a later stage. The facings need to be released, re-stuffed and permanently tacked down using 10 mm (⅜ in) fine tacks. Start by releasing all tacks on one facing only, while maintaining the tension of the scrim up the face and over the top of the back; this will help form the shape and control the size of the facing. Apply stuffing under the scrim: starting at the very top of the scroll, roll the scrim between the frame and stuffing to form the edge and permanently tack the scrim to the bevelled edge you previously prepared, ensuring that the height and overhang are achieved when the edge is stitched. After completing the curved part of the scroll, which will mean the gathering of scrim between the eight and three o'clock positions, you can now proceed onto the straight vertical section of the back. At this point assuming that you have applied the scrim correctly you should be able to continue to follow a vertical thread, which will help form an even-size edge height. In nearly all cases you will find that at each end of the edge you are forming the size of what will be the finished roll will need to be slimmed down to blend in to other upholstery. To achieve this fold the scrim in, easing it towards the scroll face and permanently tack along the bottom

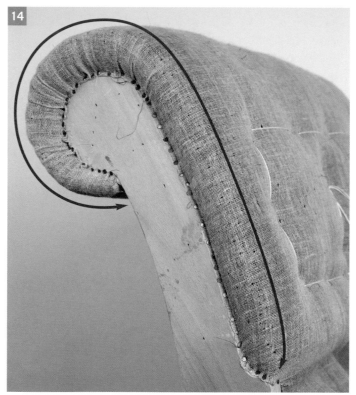

rail for approximately 10 cm (4 in). This will help form the final profile required on the front of the facing. Using the regulator and your fingers roll the remaining scrim in under the stuffing on the front facing to form, if required, a height-reducing edge. Repeat this process on the opposite facing,

ensuring that the second side is identical in size, shape and overhang to ensure the back looks balanced.

Blind and top stitching the scroll edge

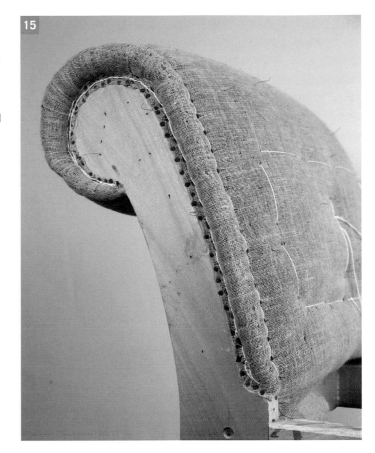

15 The number of lines of stitches required for producing a stitched roll edge depends on the height of the stuffing. In most cases this is usually one of each (one line of blind stitches and another of top stiches), and in some cases when a very small roll is required, only a top stitch is applied. The blind stitch (see page 72) should be applied by placing the needle very close to the tacks when forming the stitch; this should start the process of drawing the scrim forward to form the under-the-edge finish. When applying the top stitch (see page 72) the needle should be inserted immediately above the blind stitch and at an angle to pull the fibre-filled scrim forward, forming the roll that will become the major part of the finished overhang.

TIP: When upholstering the facings of a double-ended scroll, you can construct it by using one of two orders of construction. Examples of pros and cons for each method are listed below:

The first method is described above, where each individual stage is completed on one side, then the other.

Advantage	Disadvantage
The facings can be regularly compared with one another to ensure they are identical in density, size and shape.	When stitching it is possible to drag the scrim to one side, which could result in the roll on one side overhanging more than the other.

The second method is to complete one facing up to and including the top stitching, before releasing the opposite facing from temporary tacks.

Advantage	Disadvantage
Should the first facing overhang too much or too little, when the opposite end is released the first facing can either be drawn forward using a regulator or pulled back by pulling on the opposite side as it is re-tacked.	It is more difficult to ensure that both sides match in all aspects of the required finished shape, but more so the size of the scroll.

On completing both sides of stitching, remove/re-adjust/stuff and then permanently tack down the remaining areas on the top and bottom back rails.

Second stuffing and calico

16 A second set of bridal ties now needs to be applied over the whole surface of the back, under which hair is to be placed. The hair fills in any indentations caused by the stitching and provides the finishing shape and smoothness to the back. Ensure that the top and face of the back are correctly filled as these areas will be the most vulnerable to wear and tear.

17 A piece of calico is now required to cover the hair. Using a fabric tape, measure and cut the calico so that it is slightly larger than required. Place the calico over the back and follow the same process as the scrim, by temporary tacking the calico to the seat rail and the underside of the back rail, ensuring that the combination of the tension and the corridors is correct.

18 Sew the edge of the calico to the edge roll. To do this, pin the calico into position. Trim the calico, leaving 1.5 cm (½ in) to fold in. Remove the pins from one side of the back and, starting at the top of the scroll, fold the calico in and re-pin it. Repeat working in both directions, gently pulling the fabric down and forward to maintain the shape. On reaching both the underside of the scroll and the bottom of the back, the folded ends can be permanently tacked to the frame. The calico that is temporary fixed to the top and bottom rails can now be permanently tacked down, cutting the calico where required to the underside of the top rail and the rear of the bottom back rail.

19 The calico can now be slip stitched to the edge roll (see page 73). For the purpose of photography, a dark coloured slipping thread has been used, but you would usually use a light coloured thread.

Applying the back top fabric

20 Prior to attaching the top fabric a double layer of skin wadding must be applied over the calico to prevent the hair from piercing the fabric. The top fabric should be temporary tacked into position using the same procedure as the scrim. Once satisfied that the fabric is ready for final fixing, start by removing the tacks from one facing and trim or roll in the excess skin wadding to fill in any hollows that may have formed under the stitched roll. This will ensure a nice rounded effect on the edge. Ensure that the vertical tension on the fabric is correct; failure to do so will hinder the forming of the pleats and may result in a poor finish.

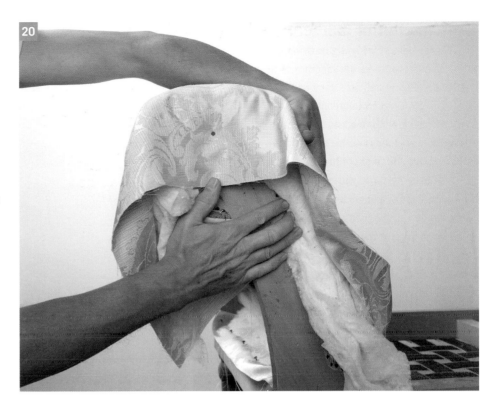

21 Start by permanently tacking the vertical side of the facing until you reach the two o'clock position on the curved scroll section. This is where you should form your first pleat. Fix the pleat into position, tacking close to the edge of the frame.

22 Continue to insert pleats around the facing until you have completed the front of the facing. Repeat the process on the other facing, matching both the number and position of pleats, while at the same time ensuring the fabric remains under tension across the back. As with the calico, the top fabric can be permanently tacked on the underside of the upper rail, but should be only temporary tacked on the rear of the bottom rail, cutting the fabric as required so that it may be moved to another rail, after the seat is completed.

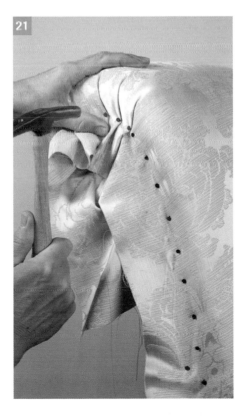

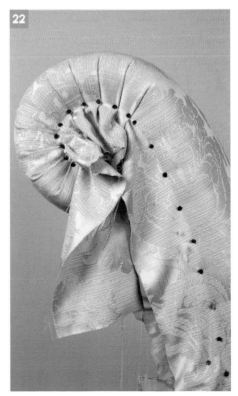

Construction of the seat

The seat is constructed using traditional springs and fillings and will incorporate all the construction techniques used on the other projects, but will introduce you to working on a larger scale and by doing so you will find that the required finish you are aiming for will be that little bit more difficult to achieve. You will need to cope with using larger amounts of fabric and that longer, straight or curved line that all upholsterers aim for will be more challenging to achieve.

Webbing the seat

23 Turn the day bed upside down making sure that it is well supported and balanced. Make sure that the upholstered back is protected and in a position in which it cannot be damaged. The whole of the underside of the seat now needs to be webbed with 5 cm (2 in) jute or black and white webbing and, on this occasion, tacked using 16 mm (⅝ in) improved tacks. Larger tacks are used here because the webs are tacked onto the underside of the frame and you need to take into account the downward force placed on them. The webs should not be placed more than half a web's distance apart, or 2.5 cm (1 in). If a wider web is used the gap between the webs should remain the same.

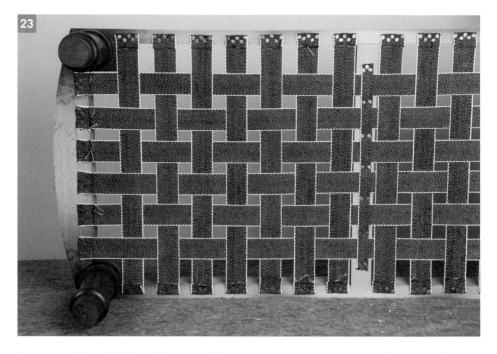

23

TIP: Applying the webbing accurately will assist in the positioning of the springs which in turn will provide you with straight lines to allow easy application of the lashing cord.

Applying the springs

24

24 Twenty-one springs (in a 7 x 3 formation) of 12.5 cm (5 in) x 10 swg springs now need to be placed into position on the webbing, taking into account the distance from the edge of the frame and the position of the upper knot. The knots on the top of the springs should face diagonally inwards and where the seat will interconnect with the back, allowing for tilt. Once satisfied with the positioning of the springs, draw round each spring with tailor's chalk or crayon so that if any are nudged while being sewn on, they can be correctly repositioned. With practice and experience you may find you will not always need to do this. As described on page 57, sew the springs to the webbing at four equal points, ensuring that the springs are secure and cannot be rotated.

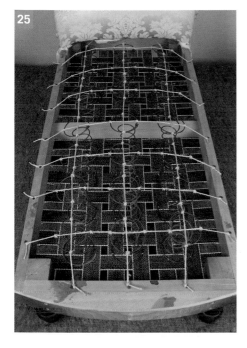

25 When all the springs have been attached to the webbing, apply a 16 mm (⅝ in) improved temporary tack opposite each line of the springs in the centre of the top surface of the rail on all four sides of the seat in preparation for lashing. Cut a length of laid cord approximately one and a half times the length of the distance across the springs from rail to rail over the top of the springs and lash the springs into position. Now repeat this operation working along the length of the seat. The length of cord required may be as much as double the finished width to take into account the number of knots to be made.

Spring hessian

26 Cover the springs with 340 g (12 oz) or heavier grade hessian, which should be applied in the same way as with Project 2 (see pages 88–95). Firstly, temporary tack the hessian into position and lose any fullness, then fold the edges and permanently tack them with 13 mm (½ in) improved tacks. The hessian should now be sewn to the springs at four points in the same way as you attached the springs to the webbing to prevent excessive wear.

Bridal ties and first stuffing

27 Apply bridal ties over the whole surface of the seat. The outer line running around the edge of the seat should be placed approximately 7.5 cm (3 in) from the edge of the frame and the remaining ties should be evenly spaced apart.

28 Always protect the top fabric, especially if it is light in colour, before applying the stuffing. Here, a plastic covering has been slipped over the back. When applying the first stuffing, start by placing the fibre at the intersection of the back and seat. The space between the back and the seat should be filled sufficiently so that no gap is visible when the scrim is applied. Other thin fillings and materials will still be required to pass through the junction of the back and seat at a later stage of construction. Continue to apply the fibre over the whole of the seat. Make sure there is sufficient fibre so that you cannot feel the springs through the stuffing but make sure you do not overstuff the seat as this will result in the seat looking like the top of a balloon rather than a gentle dome shape. The filling at the edge of the seat should be much firmer and denser than at the centre. This will help you clearly see the shape, size and height when the scrim has been completely temporary tacked into position.

Applying the scrim

29 A piece of scrim is required to cover the fibre. The scrim should be cut so that there is sufficient allowance for both setting and tacking. Place the scrim over the fibre and, following a thread, temporary tack with a small tuck along one of the long sides of the frame. Now by pulling with one hand and rubbing/manipulating with the other, ease the scrim on to the opposite side. With a small tuck temporary tack the scrim into the side of the rail, again following a thread. Before proceeding, check the corridors and also that the thread lines lie correctly. Make any adjustments necessary, then temporary tack down the open end. Prior to pushing the web between the back and seat, cuts need to be applied to allow the scrim to pass either side of the upright post.

Stuffing ties

30 Use four-cord to apply the stuffing ties (see Step 12, page 83). Here we have two separate applications of ties: one on the outer ring and one on the inner ring. Applying the ties in this way has two benefits: you will not struggle with a very long length of twine; and the ties will work independently, which in the unlikely event that one should break, the remaining ties will continue to operate as intended. This is only one of many formations that can be used. The important factor is that the correct number and spacing of the ties are used for the shape and size that you are constructing.

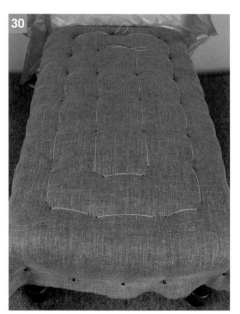

Tacking down the seat scrim

31 This seat has a wrap-over finish and, for aesthetic reasons, requires an upright edge that slightly protrudes. Start in the centre of one of the long sides and, if required, apply additional stuffing to the edge and tack down the scrim using 10 mm (⅜ in) fine tacks along the bevelled edge in preparation for stitching. The end that butts up to the back should be tacked to the end of the rail and the remaining scrim folded in to form a pleat, which can be regulated in to shape.

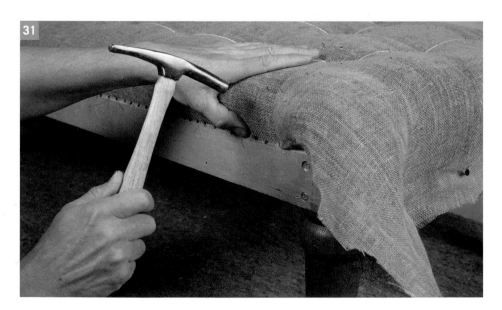

32 At the edge of the seat you should stop just short of the corner, which will allow you to form a pleat in conjunction with the end of the day bed at a later stage. Repeat this process on the opposite side of the seat. The scrim at the end of the day bed can now be re-stuffed and fixed down and in doing so where the side and end meet the corners can be formed using a single pleat. If required, the corner pleat should be stitched to hold it in place in preparation for the application of blind and top stitches.

Blind and top stitching the seat

33 The seat now requires evenly spaced blind and top stitches using four-cord (see page 72). The finished size of the stitched roll should be in the region of 2 cm (¾ in) maximum to provide a clean, sharp edge without the hard look. Start at one end close to the back and complete each line of stitching around the whole face side of the seat, before proceeding on to each additional line of stitches. On completing the stitching, permanently tack off the end that is beneath the back, checking that there is sufficient stuffing to close any gaps and ensuring a clean straight connection line between the back and seat.

Second stuffing and calico

34 Like the back, the seat will have bridal ties applied to the whole top surface area. Secure a layer of hair under the bridal ties to fill in any minor indentations caused in the construction. To achieve the final shape, which should form a gentle curve, be careful not to either under- or overstuff as this could lead to an indentation in the seating area or the feeling that the person sitting on the seat is sliding off to one side.

35 Apply calico over the hair using the same method as the scrim application. Temporary tack the calico in to place and make the required cuts. Starting on one of the long sides, release the calico one side at a time. The side should be filled with felt and/or skin wadding and permanently tacked down in a central position on the side of the rail. On completion of the first long side but stopping short at both ends, continue to the opposite side, followed by the open end finishing with single pleats on the corners and a neat pleat butting up to the back. Finally, permanently tack the calico under the back, watching for the finished line between the back and the seat.

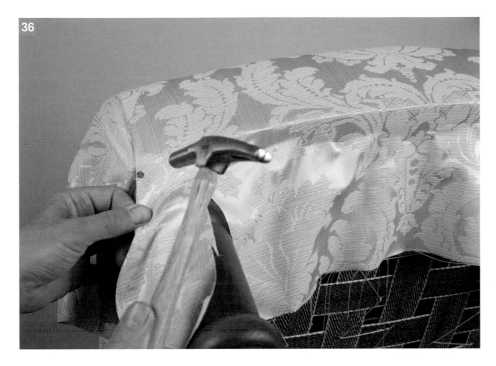

Applying top fabric to the seat

36 The top fabric should now be measured and cut for the seat, making sure that you have the correct width and length to tack on the underside of the frame and through to fix under the back. Remember to centre the pattern in line with the back; it is not always possible to pattern match at this point but positioning the pattern in such a way that it does not have two of the same parts of the design together is very important. Cover the seat with a double layer of skin wadding and temporary fix the cover into position. DO NOT make any cuts until you are totally satisfied with the position of the fabric, pattern and/or pile.

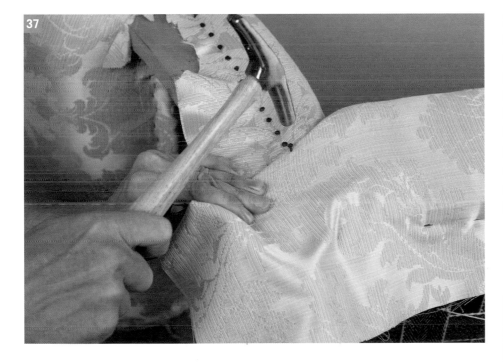

37 The fabric can now be permanently fixed following the same procedures as the calico, with one exception: note how the pleat is formed diagonally across the back to form a neat finish. When the seat fabric has been fixed, release the fabric at the bottom of the back, re-pull and tack on to the top of the seat fabric. This should close any gaps between the seat and back. Additional filling (polyester) can be applied behind the back fabric if needed.

TIP: Before trimming any excess material, stand back and examine the day bed. Check all patterns are correctly positioned, pleats are even both in height and width, and finally check that no cuts can be seen or are likely to open up during the life of the bed.

Applying the facing to the back

38 The inner surface of the back scroll requires the fabric to be fixed to form a concave effect. To do this, firstly place the pattern you made earlier on to the side of the back, lining up with the outer vertical edge of the frame, then mark and trim the pattern so it sits comfortably inside the hollow. Use this pattern to cut a piece of plywood 6, 8 or 10 mm (¼, ⁵⁄₁₆ or ⅜ in) thick (the thickness of the board is governed by how much the roll edge overhangs). The facing should now fit snugly in the space. Allowing for the thickness of fabric that will later be applied to the facing, you may need to adjust the tacks holding the back fabric to remove any infringing tacks/staples, whether they be set too far in or too far out under the facing, exposing the tack/staples.

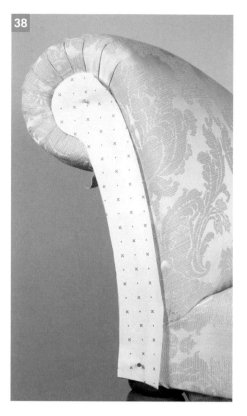

TIP: Depending on what fabric you are using, you can rub some chalk along the rear edge of the plywood facing and press it into position. Remove the facing and a chalk line will remain, enabling you to adjust the tacks/staples to allow a sung fit.

39 The edges on the front of the facing should be rounded off with glass paper, after which a layer of skin wadding or polyester 5 mm (¼ in) bigger all round should be fixed to the facing and trimmed to shape. Note the position of the staples, which are placed on the outer edge of the plywood to allow you to lift the skin wadding when fixing the facing with the nails. If the staples are incorrectly placed, the application of the facing can be affected.

40 Cut a rectangular piece of fabric 7.5 cm (3 in) wider than the largest measurements of the facing. Remember to take into account any pattern or pile on the fabric. Place the fabric right side down on to the table and lay the plywood facing over it. Holding the plywood, firmly bring the fabric over the vertical inside and staple into place. Some relief cuts may be needed were the edge is concave. Still holding the facing, cut the fabric where necessary and staple into place around the opposite vertical side and the underside of the scroll. Examine the facing and check that the tension is correct. Replace the facing back down on the work board and complete the top of the facing by gathering the excess fabric and staple in place.

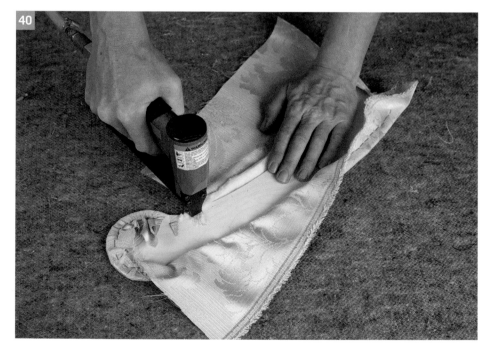

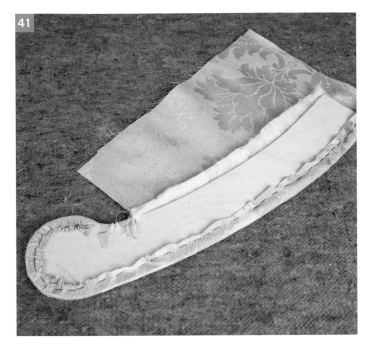

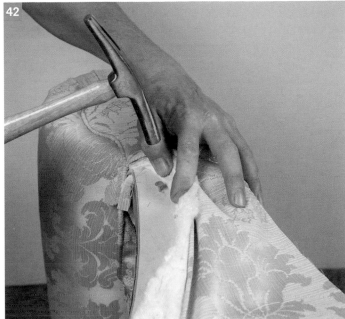

41 Double check all is correct and trim the excess fabric only where it has been stapled to the plywood. Any trim or piping should now be applied to the facing and fitted so as to allow correct positioning when the facing is applied to the frame.

42 With the bed on its side, place the facing into position on the frame and using 2.5 cm (1 in) wire nails, lift both the skin wadding and fabric that was not fixed and nail the facing to the frame with up to three nails. The top nail should be placed as high as possible beneath the facing fabric.

43 Ensure the filling is laid flat over the facing and no nails can be felt. The loose fabric can now be positioned and tacked permanently on the side of the back facing. Repeat this process to apply second facing.

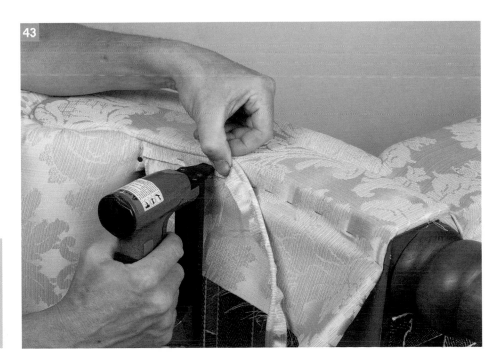

TIP: When working with mirrored facings, mark an 'X' on the back. That way you are unlikely to make the mistake of producing two facings facing the same way.

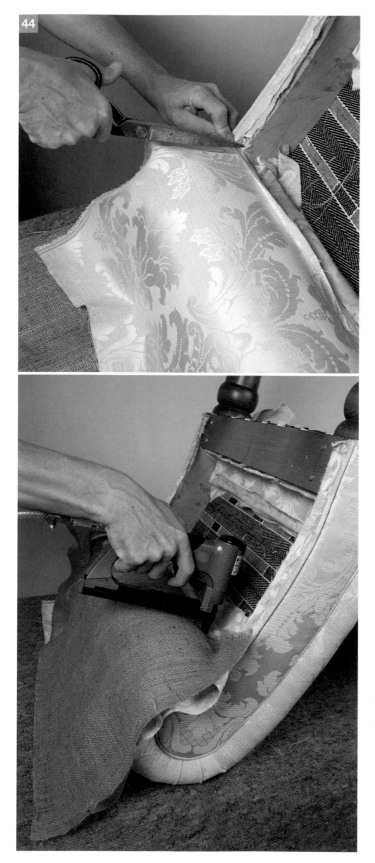

Fixing the outside back

44 The fixing of the outside back fabric follows a similar procedure to that of the outside back of the Child's chair (see pages 112–123). Start by turning the day bed upside down on the trestles, ensuring that it is well supported and padded to prevent damage to the finished areas. Taking into account any pattern or pile, cut a piece of fabric 5 cm (2 in) larger than the height and width of the back. You will also need a piece of 285 g (10 oz) hessian of the same size. Place the fabric in position on the back and make two 1.5 cm (½ in) incisions level with the inside of the frame and fix the fabric in place at each cut. Repeat this process with the hessian.

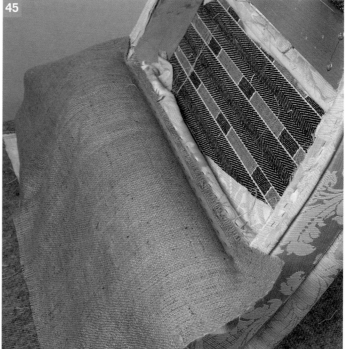

45 Cut a length of back tacking card and attach it between the rails with 13 mm (½ in) tacks or 10 mm (⅜ in) staples. The outer edge of the card should be aligned with the edge of the side post.

46 The hessian should now be folded back and tacked/stapled into place. Start by turning the hessian under and fix it to one side of the back. Applying tension to the opposite side, turn the hessian under again and fix it to the other side of the back. Finish by tacking the hessian to the lower rail to form a lining on the outside back. The hessian should then be lined with a layer of skin wadding/polyester followed by the cover which should be pinned into place on each side first. To maintain the shape, cuts are made around the legs and folded as required, then the fabric is finally eased down and tacked on the underside of the frame.

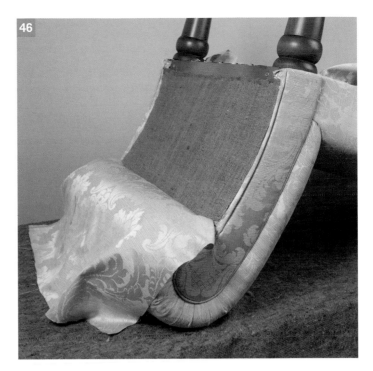

47 Slip-stitch the fabric on each side with slipping thread and a small curved needle. Choose your curved needle with care. A heavy-duty fabric may require a 7.5 cm (3 in) x 17 g needle, while a fine delicate fabric may need a 6.5 cm (2½ in) x 20 g needle.

Finally, apply bottom cloth on the underside of the day bed for a neat finish.

VARIATIONS ON STYLES OF THE BACK
This particular day bed has been constructed with an under-the-edge finish on the scrolls. Some alternative styles that could be used are:
Capped on finish: This would be constructed by machining the facings and back fabric together, using piping or decorative cord on the edge.
Deep-buttoned: For a more decorative finish the back or combination of both the seat and back could be deep buttoned, forming long, decorative diamonds throughout its length.

GLOSSARY

Algerian fibre A type of fibre used in bedding or upholstery. Palm leaves, which are shredded into filaments, are then fried and curled. It comes in the form of rope and its natural colour is green but it is boiled and dyed black to repel mites.

Antimacassar A detachable covering for backs of chairs and sofas intended to provide protection against stains.

Armchair Originally called an arming chair to distinguish it from a single or side chair, armless single chair or back stool.

Back-tacking Method of attaching a covering to conceal tacking on outside arms and arms with straight edges.

Ball and claw A carved wooden reproduction of an animal paw resting on a ball. Used decoratively as feet in furniture.

Banquette A long, continuous seat.

Bergère A Louis XIV- or XV-style chair with upholstered back and sides with squab cushion. Modern designs have cane sides and backs.

Bias cutting Cutting fabric diagonally across threads.

Bible front A bold rounded edge at the front of a seat.

Blind stitch Stitch formed with twine used to consolidate fillings.

Bolster arms A term used to describe the cylindrical arm rests of certain easy chairs because of their resemblance to bolsters.

Bottoming cloth (also known as dust cloth). A muslin cover tacked to the underside of a chair to cover webbing.

Box ottoman A divan or couch without back or arms with a hinged lid forming a seat. Mainly used for storing bedding, etc.

Border The boxing or sidewalls of a cushion or mattress.

Braid Narrow woven material used to decorate upholstery and cushions.

Bridal ties Loops of twine to hold the filling in place.

Capped on Pieces of fabric cut to shape and machined together to form a 3D cover that is capped or pulled on.

Collar Similar to a fly, but purposely shaped and sewn using the same fabric as the main panel, allowing it to mould around another shaped section of a chair, such as the arm.

Corridors A narrow band of area that runs from front to back and side to side, showing that the material is positioned correctly on a shaped area.

Fly A piece of fabric that is sewn to the top cover to extend the width and/or depth of the panel, which is hidden in the completed chair.

Facing The panel that is on the front of an arm or the side of the back.

Full seat/back A type of construction/ finish that does not require a cushion.

Fullness Excess material that accumulates when fabric is manipulated around a shape.

Genoa velvet A figured furnishing velvet with a satin base and a multicoloured pile.

Gimp Narrow woven tape used to cover tacks and raw edges on show wood furniture.

Gimp pins Fine coloured tacks with small heads, originally used to hold gimp braid in place and now occasionally used for final fixing of fabric.

Glass paper Sand paper used to smooth rough edges on frames and to clean excess glue from joints.

Gutter A channel formed in the hessian for spring edge.

Helical spring A close wound, small diameter elongated spring used in the manufacture of bedsprings.

Join A machine-stitched seam that connects two pieces of fabric.

Jute A fibre obtained from a plant grown in India used in the manufacture of webbing.

KD (Knock Down) Furniture made in separate parts for ease of transport.

Laid cord Heavy cord made from flax or hemp fibre for lashing springs. 'Laid' refers to the method of manufacture, which makes the cord stretch-resistant.

Lashing The lacing and knotting together of spring coils with heavy twine to prevent movement.

Laminated webbing Rubber webbing with rayon threads within layers of rubber.

Laths The metal straps/webs that are riveted to the bottom of single-cone springs.

Lead moulding Trimming for leather upholstery to hide tacks or gimp pins.

Lip Front edge of a cushion seat.

Mock cushion Construction of a seat to imitate a cushion which cannot be removed.

Mortise Hole cut into timber to accommodate a tenon (projection) to form a mortise and tenon joint.

Notch or notch out A very small V cut at the edge of the fabric to identify a particular point which is then lined up with a corresponding V on another piece of fabric to which it is to be joined.

Pin-stuffed Upholstery seat with only one layer of filling.

Pincers Pliers used to extract small tacks and staples from furniture frames.

Piping A cord covered with diagonally cut strips of covering or contrasting fabric. Also known as welt.

Platform Underside of a cushion (usually leather) that is not seen.

Pull-over edge A seat front with a covering pulled straight over.

Pulling point The point in a piece of fabric that is grasped and pulled, which will distort the weave and allow the fabric to mould around a shape, removing most, if not all, of the fullness.

Prie-Dieu A low-seated prayer chair with a high back. It has a narrow shelf upon which the user can rest their arms, using the seat for kneeling on.

Rebate A recess or groove cut near the edge of the frame to support a drop-in seat or to provide a tacking area.

Refurnishing Repairing or renewing.

Ripping Stripping off covering or filling from a frame.

Roll edge A roll edge prevents stuffings from working away from the edge of the frame.

Ruche Decorative trimming to hide joins in a covering.

Sash cramp A bar or pipe clamp used when re-gluing a loose joint.

Scrim Open or loosely woven fabric made from flax yarn. Used mainly for covering the first filling, such as fibre or hair.

Serpentine spring Continuous wire spring formed from zigzag strips requiring no webbing.

Show wood frame An upholstered frame with polished wood showing.

Silencer Strip of webbing or sturdy material placed between the unfastened spring coils and frame to prevent rattling when the depressed spring hits the wood.

Single-cone spring Spring with a large top coil and a tapered base.

Sinuous spring *see* Serpentine spring.

Skewers Long upholstery pins with a ring at the end.

Skirt Decorative, lined panels of fabric that are fixed around the base of a chair to form a decorative finish; an alternative to a fringe.

Skivering Shaving the underside of leather to reduce thickness.

Sofa The term appears in the late 17th century and was used to describe 'a couch for reclining' (1692).

Spring edge A flexible edge for seats or backs.

Squab Flat, firmly stuffed cushion.

Stile Part of the frame construction around which a covering must be cut.

Stitched edge A padded edge formed over the front of the spring burlap to create the desired finished shape.

Stuff over chair A chair completely stuffed over and covered.

Tack roll Method of making a soft edge on a timber frame.

Tack ties Lines in a covering due to faulty tacking.

Tacking strips Narrow chipboard strips used to reinforce tacked final covering edges.

Tailor tacks See Notch or notch out.

Tears Ripples of fabric that can form in deep buttoning.

Tenon A joinery term for a projecting end of wood shaped to fit into a corresponding cavity (mortise) in another piece of wood to form a joint.

Tension fullness A slight gathering of fabric when two or more pieces of fabric are machined together.

Terylene A man-made fibre made from oil.

Tester The top framework of a four-poster bed.

Trestle A saw horse built with padded tops and raised edges so that furniture does not slip off or get scratched.

Twine Made of flax or hemp, twine is used when applying top and blind stitches in traditional upholstery.

Under the edge Forming an overlapping roll on the front of the seat, back and arms.

Unit spring An assembly of springs to fit a seat or back.

Van-dyking Method of joining covering for diamond buttoning.

Warp Thread, parallel to the selvedge, running down the length of fabric.

Webbing Strips woven from jute fibre to provide support for filling materials.

Weft Thread running across the width of fabric.

Well Also known as a gutter, a well is a depression formed behind the first row of springs in a lashed spring seat.

Welt Better known as piping. A cord covered with diagonally-cut strips of covering or contrasting fabric. It is also commercially made.

ACKNOWLEDGEMENTS

For many years I have been encouraged to write a book on both my experience and practical knowledge of upholstery. In writing this book, I would like to acknowledge all those friends, colleagues and organisations, both in and related to the upholstery industry, that have helped me in no small way. Including those mentioned in the dedication, I would also like to add the following people and organisations, and the areas of assistance they provided in the production of this book.

Wendy Shorter, Wendy Shorter Interiors (fabric identification)
John Styles, Recticel Ltd (foams)
Mick Allen, London Metropolitan University (polishing and finishing)
Ronald Hobbs, London Metropolitan University (frames)
Ross Fabrics Ltd (sponsored fabrics)
Martins Upholstery Supplies Ltd (information)
Peter Finch, Bearsted Upholstery, Kent (sponsored materials)
London Metropolitan University (workshop and facilities)

ORGANISATIONS AND SUPPLIERS

When undertaking an upholstery project it is not always easy to obtain the specialised materials that are required. The easiest method of acquiring these materials is often a from a local established upholsterer. These and many other upholstery companies can be found in both local and national directories. The upholstery industry will use trade-only suppliers, but if contacted will often direct you to the nearest retail outlet selling their goods.

In terms of fabrics, many fabric warehouses will sell direct to the public, often offering end-of-range lines. When choosing fabrics, make sure that the fabric is suitable for the purpose required and that it meets the necessary regulations.

Here is a list of organisations and suppliers that may be of use.

Association of Master Upholsterers and Soft Furnishers
Frances Vaughan House
Q1 Capital Point
Capital Business Park
Parkway
Cardiff CF3 3PU
www.upholsterers.co.uk

Glover Brothers (trade only)
www.gloverbros.co.uk

J A Milton (retail supplier)
Ellesmere Business Park
Ellesmere
Shropshire SY12 0EW
www.jamiltonupholstery.co.uk

Martins Upholstery Supplies Ltd (trade only)
www.martinsupholserysupplies.co.uk

Upholstery Lessons and Supplies (retail supplier)
www.upholsterylessons.co.uk

INDEX